TIME
LIFE
BOOKS ®

Foods of the World

American Cooking: New England

With Supplementary Chapters on the Cooking of Eastern Canada

by

Jonathan Norton Leonard

and the Editors of

TIME-LIFE BOOKS

photographed by

Constantine Manos and Richard Jeffery

TIME-LIFE BOOKS, NEW YORK

THE AUTHOR: Jonathan Norton Leonard is an authentic New Englander by birth, brought up in East Sandwich on Cape Cod, where he still operates the family cranberry bogs. Science editor of TIME for 20 years, he now free-lances from his home in Hastings-on-Hudson, New York. His books include *Latin American Cooking,* in the FOODS OF THE WORLD library, *Planets,* in the Life Science Library and *Ancient America,* a volume in the TIME-LIFE BOOKS Great Ages of Man series.

THE PHOTOGRAPHERS: Constantine Manos *(far left)* is a New Englander by choice: born in South Carolina of Greek parentage, he is now a freelance, based in Boston. His book, *Portrait of a Symphony,* was the result of early experience as official photographer for the Boston Symphony Orchestra. He traveled widely on both sides of the border taking pictures for this volume.
 Richard Jeffery *(left),* who made the Harlow House pictures and the studio photographs, including the cover, has worked on a number of volumes for the FOODS OF THE WORLD library. Still-life materials for his photographs were selected by Yvonne McHarg.

THE CONSULTANTS: James A. Beard *(far left),* special consultant, is the leading authority on American regional foods. His many books include *Delights and Prejudices* and *The James Beard Cookbook.*
 Michael Field *(left),* consulting editor for FOODS OF THE WORLD, is a leading teacher, lecturer and writer on culinary subjects. Among his own books are *Michael Field's Cooking School, Michael Field's Culinary Classics and Improvisations* and *All Manner of Food.*

THE COVER: Corn, lobster and quahogs, or hard clams, have been delighting palates in the Northeast for centuries; the Indians were familiar with such foods long before the white man stepped ashore.

TIME-LIFE BOOKS

EDITOR: Jerry Korn
Executive Editor: A. B. C. Whipple
Planning: Oliver E. Allen
Text Director: Martin Mann
Art Director: Sheldon Cotler
Chief of Research: Beatrice T. Dobie
Picture Editor: Robert G. Mason
Assistant Text Directors: Ogden Tanner, Diana Hirsh
Assistant Art Director: Arnold C. Holeywell
Assistant Chief of Research: Martha T. Goolrick
Assistant Picture Editor: Melvin L. Scott

PUBLISHER: Joan D. Manley
General Manager: John D. McSweeney
Business Manager: John Steven Maxwell
Sales Director: Carl G. Jaeger
Promotion Director: Beatrice K. Tolleris
Public Relations Director: Nicholas Benton

FOODS OF THE WORLD

SERIES EDITOR: Richard L. Williams
EDITORIAL STAFF FOR AMERICAN COOKING: NEW ENGLAND:
Picture Editor: Iris Friedlander
Designer: Albert Sherman
Assistant to Designer: Elise Hilpert
Staff Writer: Gerry Schremp
Chief Researcher: Sarah B. Brash
Researchers: Malabar Brodeur, Marjorie Chester, Mollie E. C. Webster
Test Kitchen Chef: John W. Clancy
Test Kitchen Staff: Fifi Bergman, Sally Darr, Leola Spencer

EDITORIAL PRODUCTION
Production Editor: Douglas B. Graham
Quality Director: Robert L. Young
Assistant: James J. Cox
Copy Staff: Rosalind Stubenberg, Grace Hawthorne, Florence Keith
Picture Department: Dolores A. Littles, Joan Lynch
Traffic: Arthur A. Goldberger
Studio: Gloria duBouchet

The text for this book was written by Jonathan Norton Leonard, the recipe instructions by Michael Field and Gerry Schremp, and other material by the staff. Valuable assistance was given by these individuals and departments of Time Inc.: Editorial Production, Robert W. Boyd Jr., Margaret T. Fischer; Editorial Reference, Peter Draz; Picture Collection, Doris O'Neil; Photographic Laboratory, George Karas; TIME-LIFE News Service, Murray J. Gart; Correspondent Sue Wymelenburg (Boston).

Contents

The Recipe Booklet that accompanies this volume has been designed for use in the kitchen. It contains all of the 50 recipes printed in this book plus 106 more. It has a wipe-clean cover and a spiral binding so that it can either stand up or lie flat when open.

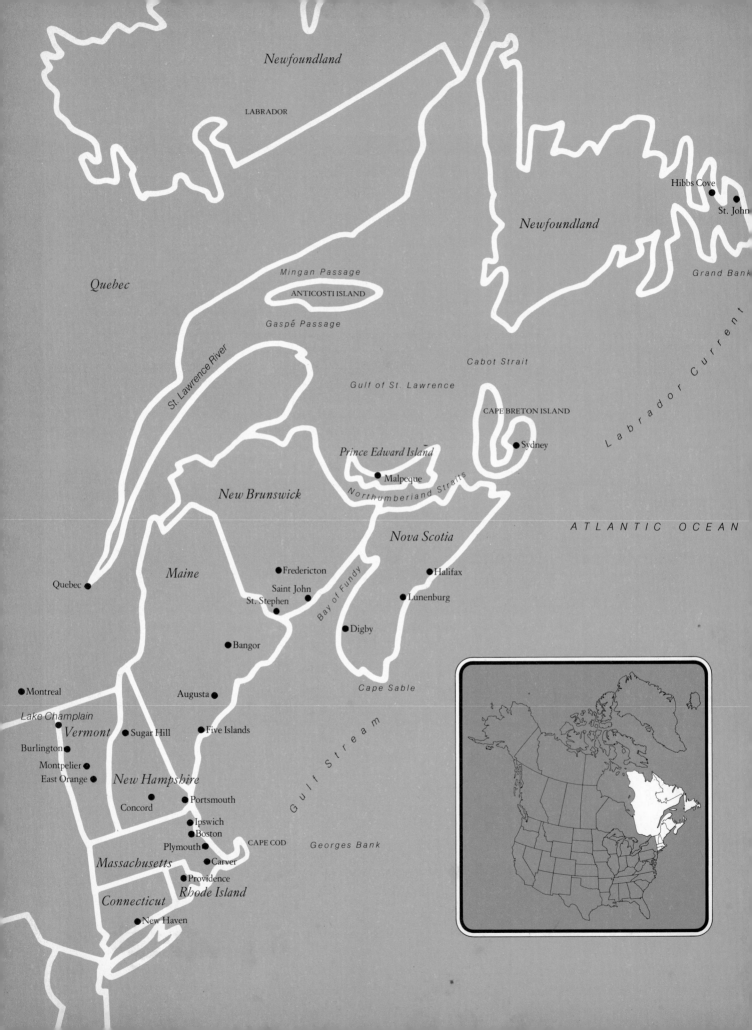

Newfoundland

LABRADOR

Newfoundland

Hibbs Cove

St. John

Quebec

Mingan Passage

ANTICOSTI ISLAND

Gaspé Passage

Grand Bank

St. Lawrence River

Gulf of St. Lawrence

Cabot Strait

Labrador Current

CAPE BRETON ISLAND

Sydney

New Brunswick

Prince Edward Island

Malpeque

Northumberland Straits

ATLANTIC OCEAN

Nova Scotia

Maine

Fredericton

Bay of Fundy

Halifax

Saint John

St. Stephen

Lunenburg

Digby

Bangor

Montreal

Augusta

Cape Sable

Lake Champlain

Vermont

Sugar Hill

Five Islands

Burlington

Gulf Stream

Montpelier

East Orange

New Hampshire

Portsmouth

Concord

Ipswich

Boston

CAPE COD

Georges Bank

Plymouth

Carver

Massachusetts

Providence

Rhode Island

Connecticut

New Haven

The Corner of the Continent
Where American Cooking Began

The map outlines the territory of this book: from well-tailored Connecticut all the way up to rough-cut Newfoundland and Labrador.

Columbus never got within 1,200 miles of here, and as a thoroughly Mediterranean man, he probably would have disliked on sight this side of the New World, rockier, chillier, and more rugged than the balmy Bahamian one he found. This is the corner of the continent where the French, a generation after Columbus, and the English, a century after that, made their tentative beachheads in America. If the winds had blown the *Santa Maria* up to Plymouth and the *Mayflower* down to San Salvador —heaven knows how history might have been changed.

Including culinary history: for (with all respect to the cuisine of New Spain) it was here in New England and in New France that the main tradition of American cooking got its start. Here the northern colonizers of the continent had to learn how to adapt their old-world kitchen traditions to such strange, new raw materials as wild turkey and corn, beans and clams, cranberries and pumpkins. They adapted well and we are all the beneficiaries of it. The foods that were developed in this part of America became and still are a principal basis of today's transcontinental fare. New England does not have the sensuous avocado, the pineapple and plantain, the tacos and tortillas that have brightened the cuisine of the southern and tropical regions of North America. Nutmegs never grew in the Nutmeg State; limes never ripened in Old Lyme, and wine grapes never thrived on Martha's Vineyard. But New England and New France offered the quahog and the sugar maple, the lobster and the crab, the bean and the cod—and the English and the French made an entirely new cuisine out of them.

The author of this book, Jonathan Leonard, writes with authority about the area and its cooking. He comes from this part of America, he understands it, loves it and knows a great deal about its food. The book is full of his delights and his prejudices—and while you may not always agree with him, he is such an expert witness that you cannot afford to disregard his opinions.

His testimony also gives evidence to what is perhaps most American about the American cuisine; it speaks eloquently of corn planted in desperation and harvested in joy, or of a feast shared by Indians and Pilgrims. As for the recipes, even their titles roll delightfully on the tongue: blueberry grunt, *bûche de Noël*, Johnston spanks, Solomon Gundy, Joe Booker stew. Best of all, their personality is every bit as pleasant to the palate.

—*The Editors*

I

Land of the Pilgrims' Pride

Looming cold and inhospitable behind the stern and rockbound coast, the forested mountains of New England seemed forbidding fortresses to the early colonists. But in time they moved inland to clear the forests and carve small farms from the rugged terrain. These sturdy old barns are in the White Mountains near Sugar Hill, New Hampshire.

For much of the 16th Century, English seamen—explorers, fur traders, fishermen—had cruised the northeast coast of America. To them it looked hostile. They feared its rocks and shoals that march far out to sea as if placed malevolently to smash the hulls of ships. They feared the fierce inhabitants of its dark forests. Most of all they feared the winter, with its blinding blizzards and biting cold so different from the clammy but gentle winter of England. Sir Ferdinando Gorges, an English soldier and courtier interested in colonization, despondently described the country as "cold and in that respect not inhabitable by our nation."

Before 1620 the only settlements were short-lived, mostly shore camps of fishermen who salted and dried their catch and fled back across the Atlantic as winter approached. But toward the end of 1620 that small, famous ship, the *Mayflower,* packed with about 100 men, women and children, wavered uncertainly toward the tip of Cape Cod. She had intended to go farther south, and why she made landfall at that barren, windswept spot is not fully known. Perhaps her captain was lost or had been deflected by the Gulf Stream, which sweeps ships northward.

In any case the Pilgrim Fathers, beset by storms and with the winter season far advanced, abandoned hope of reaching Virginia or the Hudson River, which the Dutch had explored a decade earlier. After preliminary excursions along the shore of Cape Cod they settled at what is now Plymouth, Massachusetts, on the site of a deserted Indian village. By doing so they began the creation of a new life-style. Tucked away in a part of the world that no one much coveted, they were left alone for

8

many years, free of control by the King of England or anyone else. Their survival (though half of them died the first winter) and the modest prosperity they achieved by good sense and hard work attracted from England more religious dissenters like themselves. A community, almost a nation appeared and quickly spread along the coasts and into the wild interior.

This "new" England was not much like a piece of old England. It had its own social order with local self-government, no landed aristocrats and hardly any rich or poor. It had different customs and techniques. Since houses of an English type, usually of stone, brick or "wattle and daub" (branches and mud), were not warm enough for New England winters, the colonists developed a cozier kind of house built of the plentiful local timber and constructed around an enormous central fireplace. And since many of their English farming methods did not work, they invented others that did. They adopted some new crops, such as corn, and learned new ways to raise cattle and sheep on rough, brushy pastures. They were not slaves to tradition: they were eager to try anything that looked promising, even such bizarre experiments as extracting sugar from maple trees.

Out of their innovations and adaptations came a distinctive cuisine that at its best still enchants everyone who knows it. From the beginning the Yankee cooks delighted in local products—from clams to cranberries —and devised excellent ways to present them attractively. Their religious and moral austerity did not extend to the table.

As soon as the settlers had made the necessary changes in their way of life, they found that their new land was not so bad after all. Among its granite knobs and ledges, swept bare by the great glacier of the Ice Age and never covered again in 10,000 years, were many streaks and patches of excellent soil, enough to support prosperous farms and small, neat villages. The forests were full of stately pines, some of them three feet in diameter, that made wide, knotless boards or towering ship masts. The clear, fast-running streams provided water power for grist mills and sawmills. The irregular coastline was rich in safe, deep harbors, and the cold water offshore teemed with edible sea life. Even the climate proved an asset, for New England was healthy, free of malaria and many other diseases that plagued warmer parts of the New World. The Yankees thrived, and their abounding vigor affected the whole of the future United States.

North of New England proper the settlers faced similar problems— sometimes worse ones—and made appropriate adjustments to them. The Canadian provinces of New Brunswick and Nova Scotia are rather like Maine, with the same indented coastlines and the same bare granite sticking out of the soil. Prince Edward Island is in the cold Gulf of Saint Lawrence, but by some trick of geology it escaped the touch of the glacier. It is so flat and fertile that almost every acre is carefully cultivated. At the other extreme is Newfoundland, an island about the size of Pennsylvania, far out in the Atlantic on the way to Greenland. Its interior is uninhabited, largely covered with rocks, lakes and swamps. Newfoundland lives by the sea, and its people cluster around the many snug harbors, some of them hardly more than crannies among the rocks, where hardy fishermen find shelter from the storms of the North Atlantic.

Very different is the large and populous province of Quebec, which was settled by France and is still French-speaking. It is almost three times as big as Texas, but most of its area is far northern wilderness. Its population is concentrated along the banks of the lower Saint Lawrence River. Not only its language is different from that of the English settlements; its farm houses look different, with steep roofs and eaves curved outward. The churches have steeples sheathed with zinc instead of white-painted wood, and the cultivated fields are long and narrow instead of squarish as in New England.

All these varied regions, from Connecticut to Newfoundland, have one important thing in common. All are products of adaptation to a new country. The people who adapted varied a good deal. In New England they were mostly middle-class refugees from religious persecution in England who brought their families with them. In Nova Scotia many were Gaelic-speaking farmers from the Scottish Highlands. Newfoundland was settled—so far as it has been—by several strains of fishermen; some of its people still speak with decorative Irish accents. The settlers of Quebec were almost entirely French. The first arrivals were soldiers, missionaries and adventurers rather than family men, but in contrast to the dissenting New Englanders, they were religiously orthodox. The French government permitted only certified Catholics to go to New France. Quebec is still intensely Catholic; many villages have churches that look big enough for communities 20 times their size.

The new, strange land had its effect on all newcomers. Each group developed its own ways of keeping warm and its tricks of hunting, fishing and farming, and each developed its own cuisine. There is much overlap among the regional foods. Both Vermont and Quebec, for instance, delight in maple sugar, but the uses they make of it are not all the same. Fish chowder made with milk is common to all the English-speaking sections, but Connecticut fish chowder is not much like its relatives in Nova Scotia or Newfoundland. Corn dishes are characteristic of southern New England, though corn grows in Quebec too. The coasts, naturally, have more traditional ways of serving seafood than the inland sections. Some dishes are peculiar to specific regions. Pea soup is the staff of life in French Canada while the time-honored dish of Massachusetts, baked beans, has carried Boston's name around the world.

Nearly everywhere, of course, the syndrome of the modern supermarket with its tasteless, long shelf-life breads, its chemically ripened fruit and embalmed TV dinners now lies like soggy wet newspaper over the traditional ways of cooking, but except in major industrial centers these sorry abominations are easily brushed aside. In private homes, and in an increasing number of excellent restaurants, the old regional dishes and some excellent new ones are prepared with loving skill. To sample them and trace their origin is a delightful experience.

The early development of the New England cuisine is remarkably well known, mostly because the Pilgrims at Plymouth had vivid writers among them whose records show the new way of life maturing step by step. For the first two years the Pilgrims lived barely above the starvation level. Most of these people were townsmen from London or the east of England. They arrived ill-supplied with food, and their special skills—that

Cape Cod goes back a little farther in American history than Plymouth, Massachusetts, does: in 1620 the Pilgrims spent some time around what is now Truro before sailing the *Mayflower* across the bay to establish Plymouth Colony. In time the colony expanded to include the entire area shown on the map and more; it merged with the Massachusetts Bay Colony in 1691.

of silk-weaver, for instance—were useless on the edge of the wilderness.

They had one great stroke of luck which they interpreted as an act of the Lord in their favor. A few years before the Pilgrims arrived, the Indians of southeastern Massachusetts were almost exterminated by a plague, probably some European disease to which they had little resistance. The village—Patuxet—that had occupied the site of Plymouth was depopulated; the only inhabitant who survived was a young man named Squanto who had been taken to England by explorers in 1614 and taught to speak English. He returned after the plague to find his people dead. Lost and heartbroken, he attached himself as a guide and adviser to the Pilgrims, who were making inept attempts to cultivate the abandoned Indian clearings. The plague freed Plymouth of serious Indian attack for more than a generation, while Squanto and survivors from other villages taught the Pilgrims the Indian arts of living in the new country.

The New England Indians were among the world's worst farmers, but they had a kind of agriculture that worked after a fashion. It was based on three crops—corn, beans and various sorts of squash—that they had somehow acquired by slow cultural diffusion from the centers of Indian civilization in faraway Mexico. They had never heard of Mexico but they told one of the Pilgrims, Edward Winslow, that when an Indian died his soul went south "where the beans come from."

Squanto could not have been adept at the sketchy agriculture of his people; it was mostly women's work. But he and other Indians who straggled into the English settlement taught the Pilgrims what little they knew. Their method was to prepare a patch of forest by grubbing up the un-

12

As New England settlers advanced inland along the river valleys, they built tidy villages that still delight the eye. Framed here by pine trees and maple leaves in autumn, East Orange, Vermont (founded 1781) nestles in the Waits River valley, its white clapboard houses dominated by the spire of the Union church.

dergrowth and killing the trees by girdling their trunks or burning brush piled around them. In bare places the soil was scratched with clamshell hoes and drawn together into low "hills" two or three feet apart. In the hills they planted grains of corn, and when the shoots were a few inches high, beans were planted among them so their vines could climb up the growing stalks. Pumpkins and a few other kinds of squash were also planted to trail their vines in the dappled sunlight under the corn and beans. During the summer the Indian women piled more soil around the cornstalks to keep them from blowing over. To renew the fertility of the soil they used alewives—small herringlike fish that still swim up New England streams in great numbers. They put three fish in each hill, arranged radially. This trick had the disadvantage of attracting wolves and other hungry animals that had to be shooed away.

The Indians' corn was primitive, yielding ears only four or five inches long, and it apparently had a weak root system that needed support by hilling. Modern corn is stronger and so can be planted mechanically in straight rows without hilling. But when I was a boy in Cape Cod, corn was sometimes planted in hills in the Indian way. Seven grains went into each hill, following a jingle that may have come down from Pilgrim times. It has several versions. The one I remember is:

> *One for the cutworm*
> *One for the crow.*
> *Two to perish*
> *And three to grow.*

For seed the Pilgrim used corn and beans that they had providentially found in November in an Indian cache at Truro on Cape Cod (they later located the owners and paid them for it), and in the spring of 1621 they planted the crops in the Indian manner. These crude fields thrived magnificently. The familiar harvest scene so often pictured at Thanksgiving, of corn stubble dotted with bright orange pumpkins, is Indian in origin, so it antedates even the first Pilgrim harvest in Plymouth.

While awaiting their ripening crops, the Pilgrims did not go hungry; the new land provided a bountiful if unbalanced diet. They had little fishing gear and were not good fishermen, but they did not need to be. Fish of many kinds were abundant off the shore and almost fought to be caught. Clams crowded the mudflats, and lobsters could be had for the effort of picking them up in rocky pools at low tide. Some were monsters big enough to feed four men. The Pilgrims did not like lobsters, but they admired eels. Early in Squanto's association with them he put on an exhibition of aboriginal virtuosity by catching an armful of "fatt and sweet" eels with his bare hands. Later he showed the Pilgrims how to do it.

This seafood diet, which was sometimes supplemented with wild turkey and venison, sounds luxurious but it was almost entirely protein. William Bradford, the second governor of the colony, wrote: "For food they were all alike. . . . The best dish they could present their friends with was a lobster or a piece of fish without bread or anything else except a cup of fair spring water." Not until the New Englanders developed a stable agriculture with fat and carbohydrate foods did they appreciate properly the splendid seafood that their waters produced.

During that first summer of 1621 the most reliable source of starchy food was a root called groundnut that the Pilgrims learned about from the Indians. Whenever they could not face another meal of fatless, starchless lobster or lean fish such as flounder and halibut, they could always go out and dig groundnuts, which in those days grew thick in damp places along the coast. These were not peanuts, which go by the same name in many countries, but rather the tubers of a wild bean, *Apios tuberosa,* which has almost disappeared except as a troublesome weed in cranberry bogs. The tubers look like small, fat sweet potatoes, about the size of walnuts, several strung like beads on the same thin root. Inside, they are white and crisp. When they are boiled for 15 minutes, their brown skins slip off easily, leaving the flesh soft and meaty. They taste rather like boiled chestnuts, and would find a ready sale if offered in markets; for an emergency starchy food the Pilgrims could have done much worse.

It was lucky that the Pilgrims planted a lot of Indian corn. Their English crops—wheat and peas—came to little, probably because they were varieties not adapted to the climate. The corn, however, flourished, and sometime in October the Pilgrims proclaimed a holiday (a harvest festival, though they did not call it by such a heathenish name) to celebrate their comparative plenty. Edward Winslow described this famous occasion in a letter to a friend in England: "Our harvest being gotten in, our Governor sent four men on fowling, that we might after a more special manner rejoice together, after we had gathered the fruit of our labors. The four in one day killed as much fowl as, with a little help beside, served the Company almost a week. At which time, among other recreations, we exercised our arms, many of the Indians coming among us, and amongst the rest their greatest king, Massasoit with some 90 men, whom for three days we . . . feasted. And they went out and killed five deer, which they brought to the plantation and bestowed on our Governor and upon the Captain and others."

This first Thanksgiving is often depicted as a lavish feast, with outdoor tables laden with all sorts of delicacies, but it could not have been anything of the sort. Plymouth at that time was a tiny cluster of huts, built mostly of sod and thatch. The colonists had few possessions beyond the simplest tools and household equipment, and the stores they had brought from England were practically exhausted. Most likely they entertained their Indian friends with fish and game, including the deer that the guests contributed, and corn and beans cooked in the Indian manner.

The Indians were hardly gourmet cooks. They lived so close to starvation that almost any food cooked any old way looked good to them. They made crude clay pots, which they discarded for English iron kettles as soon as they could, and their commonest cooking method was simple boiling. During the late summer and early autumn they ate a lot of boiled pumpkin (it was the first crop to ripen), and later they ate immature corn, boiling or roasting the ears while the kernels were still soft. They dried most of their corn and beans for storage through the winter. The corn was usually pounded in a mortar and cooked with water to make mush. When beans were added, the product was "succotash," the Indians' own word for it. Other foods, such as meat or fowl, could be added also. This is still done in modern Plymouth, where descendants of the Pilgrims celebrate Forefathers' Day (December 21, when the Pilgrims landed) with an elaborate stew called Plymouth succotash (*Recipe Index*). Its ingredients vary from family to family; besides corn and beans, the dish generally contains corned beef, chicken, turnips and potatoes. It is considered better on the second or third day after it is cooked, but at any time it is a magnificent meal that makes the man who has eaten it want to sleep all afternoon, or go out in a dory and row 15 miles.

The Pilgrims and the settlers who followed them to the New World kept to English cooking for the most part, but the new crops, especially corn, demanded new cookery. So little by little they found themselves adopting Indian ways of dealing with corn. They pulverized the kernels as the Indians did, often in mortars made from hollowed-out logs or stumps, with a stone pestle suspended from a bent-over sapling. The kernels were easier to reduce to meal if they were first heated or parched. The crude meal, called samp, was a mixture of coarse and fine particles. A fine corn flour could be sifted out of it, leaving a coarse remainder called hominy, also an Indian word.

The corn mush that the settlers made out of samp or hominy they named hasty pudding (*Recipe Index*) after an English oat porridge. Served for breakfast in generous helpings, it laid a firm foundation for a hard day's work. Corn meal was often carried on journeys or hunting trips by Indians and white men alike and was eaten without cooking, merely mixed into a gruel with plenty of cold water. It made a good travel ration, but no one ever praised it as a gourmet dish. Much better was

Continued on page 22

At Harlow House, Miss Rose T. Briggs, curator of the Plymouth Antiquarian Society, kneads dough for rye 'n' Injun bread—a blended loaf of rye flour and Indian corn meal which the Pilgrims often baked in the embers of the hearth. The colonists rose at dawn, and usually worked for a time before eating substantial breakfasts—such as the codfish cakes, baked beans, steamed brown bread and pitcher of ale shown at left. While the men were away working in the fields, their womenfolk spent long hours cooking at the blazing fire and their spare moments sitting at the spinning wheel, making cloth for their families.

The Bounty That Came from the Primitive Pilgrim Hearth

"She that is ignorant in cookery," ran a 17th Century proverb, "may love and obey, but she cannot cherish and keep her husband." Working over open log fires and with collections of pots hung on chains, Pilgrim wives improvised a loving bounty of robust dishes for their menfolk. A contemporary inventory of a "well-equipped" kitchen listed "6 kettles, 3 yron potts and a dripping pan. . . . 1 pair pot hangers, 2 smale old yron hookes," and included only seven plates, six spoons and three cups. The early days of austerity live on at Harlow House, built in 1677 in Plymouth, Massachusetts. Here the Plymouth Antiquarian Society has created a living museum where local women in Pilgrim costumes occasionally prepare traditional Pilgrim feasts for the public—such as beans and fish cakes for breakfast.

At the great hearth of Harlow House, Miss Briggs prepares a festive Pilgrim meal. On the hearthstone, from left, are stewed pumpkin (in the small pot), rye 'n' Injun bread, cranberry sauce and roast duck. Hanging in kettles are succotash *(left)* and steamed clams. Usually, drippings from the ducks were saved to make gravy. Everything was prepared over the fire except the bread, which was baked in the brick oven at top left.

Overleaf: The feast is spread out on the fire-room table, with an extra dish of chicken and corned beef chunks *(center)* taken from the succotash, a big bowl of Indian pudding *(right)*, a pewter pitcher of cider, and wooden bowls and mugs. The Pilgrims ate informally, for there were rarely enough chairs or utensils. This spread includes a few knives and spoons, but no forks. Often parents would feed the children from their own plates.

jonnycake (journey cake), a dry corn bread made of scalded meal and either baked or fried *(Recipe Index)*. It was just as good at the end of a journey as at the beginning. When made of commercially ground meal and baked thin with butter in the mix it is delicious and should be made more often by modern cooks.

Besides the various things they made out of cornmeal, the settlers adopted another Indian trick with corn. When dry corn kernels are soaked in the leachings of wood ashes (which contain alkaline potash), they swell up; the skins loosen and are easily rubbed off. Then the kernels are simmered for four hours until they are soft and fluffy. The result is hulled corn (sometimes called big, lye, or whole hominy). It can be made with soda or lye instead of wood ashes, and the best corn to use is white.

Back when Cape Cod was not the swarming summer resort that it is today, I remember the hulled-corn man peddling his fresh product from door to door and selling it by the quart. I have not seen this welcome visitor for many years, but hulled corn is not extinct. A few New Englanders still make it by the old-fashioned method, and it can be bought in cans. It is excellent when served hot for breakfast with butter, and for other meals it provides an interesting alternative to potatoes, noodles or rice.

Neither the Yankee hulled-corn men nor the Indians who taught them their art could have known where this unusual food originally came from. It was invented somewhere in Mexico perhaps 2,000 years ago. Hulled corn is the same as *nixtamal,* the soaked corn kernels that the Aztecs included in their chili-hot stews or ground to make their tortillas.

Another technique of the Indians is probably even more ancient: their way of cooking clams and other bulky shellfish that are hard to boil or steam in sufficient quantity in small pots. Indians who lived along the seashore commonly went out in the morning and built a fire on a layer of stones. By the time they had dug a sufficiency of clams, the wood had burned away and the stones were hot. They covered the stones with wet seaweed, spread the clams on this and covered the clams with another layer of seaweed. Then they sat back and let the steam open and cook the clams. This primitive method was practiced by the Indians of both North and South America from earliest times and used for many kinds of food. For clams it is superb: no other way of cooking them makes them taste as good. So the archaic Indian clambake flourishes to this day.

Except for migratory wildfowl, which were enormously plentiful and easily killed with the crude matchlock guns of the time, the first settlers ate little meat. They were not skilled hunters; hardly any middle-class Englishmen were. Nearly all the game in England at the time was enclosed in carefully guarded hunting preserves whose aristocratic owners saw to it that poachers were savagely punished. Most of the venison, moose meat and bear meat that the settlers got was killed by Indians.

This situation did not last long. Cattle brought from England adapted themselves to the new country and multiplied rapidly. (The vanguard, three cows and a bull, reached Plymouth in 1624.) They were not the pampered milk machines of modern dairy farms, which demand delicate food and snug shelter. Cows in those days were almost wild animals that could digest practically anything green, or that had once been green, and make milk out of it. They could even eat the tough grasses and seeds of the tidal salt marshes. These marshes, then called "meadows," were highly valued and carefully mowed for hay when the tide was down. Their only value now is as scenery, but the author has a dim childhood memory of rounded haystacks dotting the Barnstable marshes on Cape Cod, each perched on a cluster of posts so high water would not carry the hay away. Perhaps a few cows with old-style digestive apparatus still survived in Barnstable then, but more likely the harsh salt hay was sold for some other purpose than cattle fodder.

As soon as cattle became fairly plentiful, in about 1640, most of the basic ingredients of New England cooking were available. Cattle not only supplied beef, milk, butter and cheese; they also supplied oxen with which farmers could pull stumps, harrow or plow the stubborn, root-filled soil and reduce the land to cultivated fields in which English crops would grow. Corn was never abandoned, but wheat and rye took their places beside it. Chickens scurried around the crude barnyards and hogs rooted for food where they could find it. Fruit trees brought as slips from England grew fast and bore well. In a single generation New England became a stable farming community well supplied with most of the foods its people had known in England, and many indigenous foods as well.

Now its housewives could elaborate their new cuisine, and this they did with a will. At first they had only the simplest cooking utensils. Their stove was an open fireplace built initially of stone and mud, later of brick and mortar. The most important utensil—in some households the only one—was an iron kettle with a bail and hook that permitted it to be hung on the lug pole over the fire. The lug pole was made of green wood so it would not catch fire readily, but it had to be checked frequently lest it burn through and give way, dumping the dinner in the fire and scalding the children, who often squatted nearby for warmth.

When iron became more plentiful in the colony, the dangerous lug pole was replaced by the swinging iron fireplace crane, provided with hooks of various lengths so a pot could be made to boil vigorously by hanging it directly in the flames or to simmer gently by hanging it higher. More important for the housewife was the crane's ability to swing outward into the kitchen. Now she could look into the pot and tell how the dinner was doing without poking her head over the fire. The crane did as much for the housewives of the 17th Century as gas and electric ranges have done for those of the 20th Century.

When a family possesses no more than one or two iron kettles hung over an open fire, it learns to make multiple use of them. The biggest kettle was generally kept busy heating water for washing dishes and other household purposes. But this did not mean that it did not have other duties too. All sorts of things were suspended for heating or steaming in its boiling water. New England brown bread, which is steamed instead of baked, was ideal for the frontier house with a fireplace and a kettle but no oven. A tin mold of corn and whole-wheat batter was suspended in the kettle of boiling water and left there for a few hours. The tin was not indispensable; if the batter was simply enclosed in a pudding cloth, it could cook indefinitely without much effect on the water around it in the

kettle. Other combinations were possible. While the kettle was cooking tough meat for a stew, it could also cook a sweet pudding in a cloth bag. The flavors did not swap around appreciably.

Frying, which became possible as soon as the settlers obtained pigs and lard, was done in a cast-iron pan with a long handle and three legs to hold it above the coals and ashes on the hearth. There were also similar round-bottomed pans, rather like the woks of Chinese cookery, in which small amounts of food could be warmed up quickly.

Baking required more elaborate equipment. Minor matters such as baking powder biscuits and jonnycake were baked in straight-sided iron kettles that stood on tripods as the frying pans did and had covers with raised rims. They were set on a bed of glowing coals, and more coals were heaped on the cover so the contents would get heat from both above and below. (This was the ancestor of the Dutch ovens that are still used by modern campers who do not depend on kerosene or propane camp stoves.) In later colonial kitchens the heat to brown the tops of biscuits was provided by a sheet of bright tin placed in front of the fire to reflect the heat back upon them.

All these devices called for considerable skill as well as constant attention, but the real test of a 17th Century cook was the brick oven in which she did her serious baking. In the early years the oven was a simple brick box built into one side of the great open fireplace. To fire it up it was filled with fine-cut kindling wood. When this had burned partly down, solid logs were added. The oven had no separate flue; its smoke (that which did not get into the kitchen) went up the main chimney.

While performing her numerous other duties, the housewife kept an eye on the flaming oven. When the brickwork on top turned a lighter color, which meant it was hot enough to burn off the soot within the oven, she knew it was ready for baking. Then she raked out the coals and ashes and put in her loaves of bread, whose rising she had timed to match the heating of the oven. This was done with a long-handled iron (sometimes a wooden) "peel," a shovellike implement with a flat blade big enough to carry a bread loaf. Bread and other foods that required long baking went into the oven first while pies, cakes and cookies were put in front so they could be taken out sooner. When the oven was full it was closed with a heavy wooden hingeless door, closely fitted and made so that its inner surface could be renewed when it got too charred.

Managing this primitive oven with the main fire blazing close by must have been a difficult and sometimes dangerous chore, with a good chance of burning oneself or setting long skirts on fire. When the New England settlements became prosperous and more elaborate houses were built, the brick oven was moved outside the main fireplace and given a flue of its own and a swinging iron door that had a damper to control the flow of air and the speed of baking. Ovens of this more convenient type persisted long after the iron cookstove was invented. Many an excellent cook insisted that there was nothing like an open hearth and a brick oven to produce the traditional foods that her menfolk demanded.

Though cooking was an arduous business, the good colonial housewife had many other duties besides. She generally tended the important veg-

Opposite: Joe Booker stew makes a robust meal of beef simmered with rutabagas, potatoes and carrots and topped with parsley-flavored dumplings. Today no one recollects who Joe Booker was, but a steaming bowl of his namesake stew is still favored around Boothbay Harbor, Maine, where howling winter gales can chill a man to the bone.

etable garden, or worked just as hard to make her children do it. She took care of the chickens. In odd moments she spun linen or wool thread and wove it into cloth. And from late summer onward she was thinking about the coming winter and making provision for it. The New Englanders were nothing if not provident, and for the scattered farmhouses either in villages or deep in the ragged remnants of the great forest there were no markets of any kind. A few foods, such as sugar, molasses and spices, were imported, and a few others were obtained by barter with other settlers. Everything else was the produce of the land or its waters, and it had to be gathered, stored and preserved for the long winter.

In those days "preserving" was not a ladylike matter of putting up a few dozen jars of jelly or jam. It was a serious, almost a life-and-death matter. While the men did the heaviest work, getting in the hay and grain and cutting the great stacks of firewood that would keep the house warm through the winter, the women were as busy as squirrels tucking nuts in a hollow tree. Cucumbers and other vegetables were made into pickles. Animals that could not be kept through the winter were slaughtered; some of the meat was salted in barrels of brine. Some was hung in the chimney to smoke. Root vegetables such as potatoes, turnips and beets were stored in the cellar. Dry beans went into the attic along with dried apples, dried pumpkin and a variety of dried herbs. Surplus milk was made into cheese, and all except the best apples went to make fermented hard cider, the common alcoholic drink of early New England.

All this preserving, salting and drying had a considerable effect on the New England cuisine by creating a taste for the dishes it made possible. The corned beef that figures in many recipes, for instance, was originally the surplus meat packed of necessity into the farmer's salt barrel for winter eating. Salt pork had the same origin and even more uses. Dried salt codfish, which could keep for several winters, was a staple near the long coastline and a good way inland. It had a flavor all its own, not at all like fresh fish, and several excellent dishes were made from it. They are still made today in homes that appreciate this centuries-old product. I remember with the greatest pleasure the codfish cakes I had for breakfast as a child, the codfish with egg-and-cream sauce and the Cape Cod version of the New England boiled dinner, which had salt pork scraps and salt codfish as its centerpiece instead of corned beef.

Dried apples were common everywhere until they were driven off the winter market by fresh and canned fruits. Many people, including myself, considered dried apple pie to be better than fresh apple pie. It had a different and more authoritative taste. Farm families dried their own apples; some of them organized "apple-paring bees" to help make the chore a pleasure. Dried apples could be bought from neighbors or from peddlers, and many stores carried them. The ones I remember were light tan rings with a leathery feel and a sharp sweet-acid taste. I loved them as a kind of candy but was warned not to eat too many. A horrible tale was circulated in the youngest set. If a boy, so went the cautionary tale, ate too many dried apples, he would be assailed by a frightful thirst. Driven uncontrollably to the kitchen pump, he would drink glass after glass of water. The apples inside him would swell, and the poor boy would burst.

Plymouth Succotash

Wash the fowl thoroughly inside and out under cold running water; remove and discard any chunks of fat from the cavity. Truss the bird securely with kitchen string and place it in a 12-quart pot. Add the corned beef brisket and 4 quarts of water. The water should cover the fowl and brisket by about 1 inch; if necessary, add more water.

Bring to a boil over high heat, meanwhile skimming off the foam and scum that rise to the surface. Add the carrots, the clove-pierced onion, the celery stalk and a parsley-and-bay leaf bouquet. Reduce the heat to low and simmer partially covered for about 2 hours, or until the fowl is tender and shows no resistance when a thigh is pierced deeply with the point of a small knife. Then transfer the fowl to a plate. Cover and simmer the brisket for about 1 hour longer until it, too, is tender.

With a small, sharp knife, remove and discard the skin and bones from the fowl. Then cut the meat into 1-inch pieces and set aside. Transfer the brisket to a plate and cut it into 1-inch cubes. Strain the broth through a fine sieve into a deep bowl and skim as much fat as possible from the surface. (There should be about 3 quarts of broth.)

Meanwhile, prepare the beans in the following fashion: In a heavy 4- to 5-quart casserole, bring 2 quarts of water to a boil over high heat. Drop in the dried beans and boil them uncovered for about 2 minutes. (The water should cover the beans by at least 2 inches; if necessary, add more water.) Turn off the heat and let the beans soak for 1 hour. Then add a clove-pierced onion, a second parsley-and-bay leaf bouquet and 2 teaspoons of salt and bring to a boil again.

Reduce the heat to low, partially cover the pan and simmer the beans for about 1 hour, or until they can be easily mashed against the side of the pan with a spoon. (Check the beans from time to time as they simmer and add more boiling water if needed.) Drain the beans through a fine sieve set over a bowl and reserve the cooking liquid. Pick out and discard the onion and the bouquet, then transfer the beans to a separate bowl and mash them to a smooth paste with a fork.

Pour 4 cups of the chicken-and-brisket stock into a 3- to 4-quart enameled or stainless-steel saucepan, and bring to a boil over high heat. Drop in the rutabaga and cook briskly, uncovered for 25 to 30 minutes until it is tender. Drain in a sieve or colander set over a bowl.

Measure the rutabaga cooking liquid and pour it into a heavy 8- to 10-quart casserole. Add enough chicken-and-brisket stock to make 8 cups of liquid in all. Then add the rutabaga, the mashed beans and the canned hominy and, stirring constantly, bring to a boil over high heat. Reduce the heat to low and simmer partially covered for 30 minutes.

Stir in the pieces of chicken and beef, cover partially and simmer for 30 minutes longer. Check the pan from time to time and, if the mixture seems dry, add more of the meat stock or, if you have used it all, add as much of the bean stock as you need. When finished, the succotash should be thick, with most of the liquid in the pan evaporated. Taste for seasoning and serve at once, mounded on a deep platter or in a large bowl.

To serve 10 to 12

CHICKEN AND CORNED BEEF
A 5- to 6-pound stewing fowl
A 3- to 4-pound corned beef brisket
4 quarts water
2 large carrots, scraped
1 large onion, peeled and pierced with 3 whole cloves
1 celery stalk, including the green leaves
4 sprigs fresh parsley and 1 medium-sized bay leaf tied together with kitchen string

BEANS
2 to 3 quarts water
2 cups (1 pound) dried pea beans
1 large onion, peeled and pierced with 3 whole cloves
4 sprigs fresh parsley and 1 medium-sized bay leaf tied together with kitchen string
2 teaspoons salt

1 pound rutabaga, peeled and cut into 1-inch cubes
Two 1-pound, 4-ounce cans whole-kernel hominy

1 With the drumsticks pointing at the knife hand, cut deeply between one thigh and the body of the bird.

2 Press the thigh firmly against the platter with the carving fork and ease the leg away from the body.

3 Sever the thigh from the body of the bird at the exposed joint and lift the leg onto another plate.

  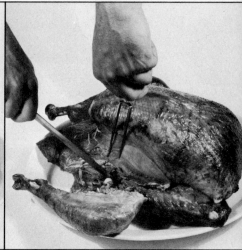

4 Hold the thigh in place with the fork and cut the drumstick from it at the joint in the leg.

5 Carve the meat from the thigh for easy serving by slicing it lengthwise, parallel to the bone.

6 Remove the wing from the same side, pulling it away from the body to locate and cut through the joint.

7 Carve the breast meat in two stages to avoid overlarge pieces. First cut thin slices from the neck end, holding the blade parallel to the breastbone.

8 Then carve a second group of slices from the top part of the breast. To carve the other half of the bird, keep it in position and repeat the procedure.

Boston Brown Bread

In a deep bowl, beat the buttermilk and molasses together vigorously with a spoon. Stir in the raisins. Combine the rye flour, whole-wheat or graham flour, corn meal, soda and salt and sift them into the buttermilk mixture 1 cup at a time, stirring well after each addition.

Thoroughly wash and dry two empty 2½-cup (No. 2) tin cans. Then, with a pastry brush, spread the softened butter over the bottom and sides of the cans. Pour the batter into the cans, dividing it evenly between them. The batter should fill each can to within about 1 inch of the top. Cover each can loosely with a circle of buttered wax paper and then with a larger circle of heavy-duty aluminum foil. The foil should be puffed like the top of a French chef's hat, allowing an inch of space above the top edge of the can so the batter can rise as it is steamed. Tie the wax paper and foil in place with kitchen string.

Stand the cans on a rack set in a large pot and pour in enough boiling water to come about ¾ of the way up the sides of the cans. Return the water to a boil over high heat, cover the pot tightly, and reduce the heat to low. Steam the bread for 2 hours and 15 minutes. Remove the foil and paper from the cans at once, and turn the bread out on a heated platter if you plan to serve it immediately. Or leave the bread in the cans with the foil and paper in place, and steam it for 10 to 15 minutes to reheat the loaves before you serve them. Steamed loaves, with covers in place, can safely be kept in the refrigerator for a week to 10 days.

NOTE: If rye and whole-wheat flours are not available at your grocery, you can find them in a health food store.

To make two 5½-by-3-inch cylindrical loaves

2 cups buttermilk
¾ cup dark molasses
¾ cup seedless raisins
1 cup rye flour
1 cup whole-wheat or graham flour
1 cup yellow corn meal
¾ teaspoon baking soda
1 teaspoon salt
1 tablespoon butter, softened

Steamed Clams

Wash the clams thoroughly under cold running water, discarding any with broken shells as well as those whose necks do not retract when prodded gently with a finger.

In an 8- to 10-quart steamer or casserole, melt the 4 tablespoons of butter bits over moderate heat. When the foam begins to subside, add the onions and, stirring frequently, cook for about 5 minutes. When the onions are soft and translucent, stir in the parsley and 3 cups of water and bring to a boil over high heat. Add the clams, cover tightly, and steam for 5 to 8 minutes, turning them about in the pot once or twice with a slotted spoon. All the shells should open; discard any clams that remain shut.

With tongs or a slotted spoon, transfer the clams to a deep heated platter or serving bowl. Strain the broth remaining in the steamer through a sieve lined with a double thickness of damp cheesecloth and set over a bowl. Pour the broth into 4 heated soup cups and serve the melted butter separately in individual bowls.

To eat a steamed clam, remove it from the shell with a small fork or your fingers, dip it into the broth to moisten the clam and remove any trace of sand, and then immerse it in the melted butter.

NOTE: Though steamers taste best when fresh, they can be safely kept in the refrigerator for 2 or 3 days. Place them in a bowl or pan and store them uncovered so that the clams can breathe. Do not wash them until you are ready to steam them.

To serve 4

8 dozen steamer or small soft-shell or long-neck clams (see page 90)
4 tablespoons butter, cut into ½-inch bits, plus ½ pound butter, melted
½ cup finely chopped onions
2 tablespoons finely chopped fresh parsley
3 cups water

Codfish Balls

To make about 30 two-inch balls

1 pound salt cod
6 medium-sized boiling potatoes (about 2 pounds), peeled and quartered
8 tablespoons butter, softened and cut into ½-inch bits
3 egg yolks
1½ teaspoon Worcestershire sauce
1 teaspoon dry English mustard
½ teaspoon ground white pepper
Vegetable oil for deep frying

Starting a day ahead, place the cod in a glass, enameled or stainless-steel pan or bowl. Cover it with cold water and soak for at least 12 hours, changing the water 3 or 4 times.

Drain the cod, rinse it under cold running water, place it in a saucepan and add enough fresh water to cover the fish by 1 inch. Bring to a boil over high heat. (Taste the water. If it seems very salty, drain, cover with fresh water and bring to a boil again.) Reduce the heat to low and simmer partially covered for about 20 minutes, or until the fish flakes easily when prodded gently with a fork. Drain the cod, remove and discard any skin and bones, and shred the fish into fine flakes with a fork.

Meanwhile, drop the potatoes into enough boiling water to cover them completely. Boil briskly uncovered until the potatoes are soft and crumble easily when pierced with a fork. Drain off the water and return the pan of potatoes to low heat. Slide the pan back and forth over the heat for a minute or so until the potatoes are completely dry.

Purée the potatoes through a food ricer set over a deep bowl, or place them in the bowl and mash them to a smooth purée with a potato masher or electric mixer. Add the flaked cod, butter bits and egg yolks to the purée and beat them vigorously together with a wooden spoon. Beat in the Worcestershire sauce, mustard and pepper. Taste for seasoning.

Preheat the oven to its lowest setting. Line a large shallow baking dish with paper towels and place it in the center of the oven.

Pour vegetable oil into a deep fryer or large, heavy saucepan to a depth of 3 inches and heat the oil to a temperature of 375° on a deep-frying thermometer. To make each codfish ball, drop a heaping tablespoon of the cod mixture into the hot oil. Fry the balls 5 or 6 at a time for about 4 minutes, or until they are golden on all sides. As they brown, transfer them to the lined pan and keep them warm in the oven while you fry the rest.

Serve the codfish balls hot, mounded attractively on a heated platter and accompanied if you wish by cole slaw, presented in a separate bowl.

Harlow House Baked Beans

To make about 3 quarts

2 to 3 quarts water
4 cups (2 pounds) dried pea or Great Northern beans
1 large onion, peeled, plus 2 large onions, peeled and each pierced with 2 whole cloves
1 teaspoon plus 1 tablespoon salt
¾ cup dark molasses
¾ cup dark brown sugar
1 tablespoon dry mustard
1 teaspoon freshly ground black pepper
½ pound salt pork in one piece, with rind left on

In a heavy 4- to 5-quart casserole, bring 2 quarts of water to a boil over high heat. Drop in the dried beans and boil them for about 2 minutes. (The water should cover the beans by at least 2 inches; add more if necessary.) Turn off the heat and let the beans soak for 1 hour. Then add the peeled onion and 1 teaspoon of salt and bring to a boil again. Reduce the heat to low, partially cover the pan and simmer for about 1 hour, or until the beans are tender. Check from time to time and add more boiling water to the pot if necessary. (The beans should be covered with water throughout the cooking.) Drain the beans through a fine sieve set over a bowl, pick out and discard the onion and reserve the cooking liquid. There should be about 2 quarts of liquid; add water if necessary.

In a deep bowl, mix the molasses, ½ cup of the brown sugar, the mustard, 1 tablespoon of salt and the pepper. Pour in about ½ cup of the bean liquid and stir to blend the ingredients well. Stir in the remaining bean liquid, then add the beans and turn them about gently with a spoon until they are evenly coated.

Preheat the oven to 200°. Place the clove-pierced onions in the bottom of a 4- to 5-quart bean pot and ladle the bean mixture over them. Score the fatty side of the salt pork by making crisscrossing diagonal cuts about ½ inch deep and ½ inch apart all over the surface. Push the salt pork down into the beans, letting only the top edge protrude above them. Cover the pot with a piece of foil and set the lid securely in place.

Bake the beans in the middle of the oven for 7 hours. Then remove the lid and foil, spread the remaining ¼ cup of brown sugar evenly over the beans and bake for 1 hour longer. Serve the beans at once, directly from the pot. Leftover beans may be refrigerated in the same pot; tightly covered with foil or plastic wrap, they can safely be kept for a week to 10 days. The beans will absorb the cooking liquid as they stand; add a little more water to the pot before reheating them in the oven.
(Adapted from a recipe in *The Plimoth Colony Cook Book*.)

Joe Booker Stew

In a heavy 12-inch skillet at least 3 inches deep, fry the salt pork dice over moderate heat, turning them about frequently with a slotted spoon until they are crisp and brown and have rendered all their fat. Remove the pork bits and discard them.

Add the onions to the fat in the skillet and, stirring frequently, cook for 8 to 10 minutes, or until they are soft and delicately brown. With a slotted spoon, transfer the onions to a bowl and set aside.

Pat the beef cubes completely dry with paper towels, roll them in ¼ cup of flour to coat them on all sides and shake off the excess flour. Brown 6 or 7 cubes at a time in the hot fat remaining in the skillet, turning them with a slotted spoon and regulating the heat so that they color evenly without burning. As they brown, add the cubes to the onions.

Pour 1 cup of water into the skillet and bring to a boil over high heat, stirring constantly and scraping in the brown particles that cling to the bottom and sides of the pan. Return the onions and beef and the liquid that has accumulated around them to the skillet. Add the remaining 5 cups of water, the parsley and bay leaf, the thyme, salt and a liberal grinding of pepper. Bring to a boil over high heat, reduce the heat to low, cover tightly and simmer for 1 hour. Stir in the potatoes, carrots and rutabaga, cover again and simmer for 30 minutes longer.

Meanwhile prepare the parsley dumplings in the following fashion: Combine the 2 cups of flour, baking powder and ½ teaspoon of salt and sift them into a deep bowl. Add the butter bits and, with your fingers, rub the flour and fat together until they look like flakes of coarse meal. Add the milk and chopped parsley and beat vigorously with a spoon until the dumpling mixture is smooth.

Remove the parsley and bay leaf from the simmering stew, and drop the dumpling mixture on top by the heaping tablespoon. Cover tightly and simmer undisturbed for about 10 minutes longer. The dumplings are done when they are puffed and fluffy, and a cake tester inserted in the center of a dumpling comes out clean.

Remove the dumplings and transfer the stew to a preheated bowl or deep platter. Arrange the dumplings on top and serve at once.

To serve 6

STEW
½ pound lean salt pork, cut into ¼-inch dice
4 medium-sized onions, peeled and cut crosswise into ¼-inch slices (about 1½ cups)
2 pounds lean beef chuck, trimmed of excess fat and cut into 1-inch cubes
¼ cup flour
6 cups water
4 sprigs fresh parsley and 1 small bay leaf tied together with kitchen string
⅛ teaspoon crumbled dried thyme
2 teaspoons salt
Freshly ground black pepper
2 medium-sized boiling potatoes, peeled and cut into ½-inch cubes (about 2 cups)
12 medium-sized carrots, scraped and cut into ½-inch pieces (about 2 cups)
1 medium-sized white rutabaga, peeled and cut into ½-inch cubes (about 1 cup)

PARSLEY DUMPLINGS
2 cups flour
1 tablespoon double-acting baking powder
½ teaspoon salt
2 tablespoons butter, cut into ½-inch bits and softened
1⅓ cups milk
¼ cup finely chopped fresh parsley

31

To serve 8

A 12-pound turkey, thoroughly
    defrosted if frozen
2 teaspoons plus 1 tablespoon salt
The neck, gizzard, heart and liver
    of the turkey
1 medium-sized carrot, scraped and
    cut into 1-inch lengths
1 small onion, peeled and quartered
4 sprigs fresh parsley
1 small bay leaf
4 cups water
2 one-pound loaves of day-old
    homemade-type white bread,
    trimmed of crusts and torn into
    ½-inch pieces (about 10 cups)
¾ cup finely chopped fresh parsley
2 tablespoons finely grated fresh
    lemon peel
1 tablespoon crumbled dried sage
    leaves
½ teaspoon freshly ground black
    pepper
½ pound butter, cut into ½-inch
    bits plus 8 tablespoons butter,
    softened
3 cups finely chopped onions
2 cups finely chopped celery
1½ pints shucked oysters (3 cups)
    drained
1 egg, lightly beaten
3 tablespoons flour

Roast Turkey with Oyster Stuffing

Pat the turkey completely dry inside and out with paper towels. Rub the cavity with 1 teaspoon of the salt and set the bird aside.

Before making the stuffing, combine the turkey neck, gizzard, heart and liver, the carrot, quartered onion, parsley sprigs, bay leaf, 1 teaspoon of salt and the water in a 3- to 4-quart saucepan. Bring to a boil over high heat, reduce the heat to low and simmer partially covered for 1½ hours.

Strain the liquid through a fine sieve into a bowl and reserve it. (There should be about 2 cups of turkey stock; if necessary, add enough fresh or canned chicken stock for the required amount.) Remove the liver, chop it into ¼-inch dice and reserve. Discard the rest of the turkey pieces as well as the vegetables and herbs.

Meanwhile preheat the oven to 400°. Combine the bread, chopped parsley, lemon peel, sage, 1 tablespoon of salt and the pepper in a large deep bowl and toss with a spoon until well mixed.

In a heavy 10- to 12-inch skillet, melt the ½ pound of butter bits over moderate heat. When the foam begins to subside, add the chopped onions. Stirring frequently, cook for about 5 minutes until they are soft and translucent but not brown.

Stir in the celery and cook for a minute or so; then, with a rubber spatula, scrape the entire contents of the skillet into the bread mixture. Add the oysters and egg and stir the ingredients gently but thoroughly together. Taste the oyster stuffing for seasoning.

Fill both the breast and the neck cavity of the turkey with the stuffing and close the openings by lacing them with small skewers and kitchen cord, or sewing them with heavy, white thread. Truss the bird securely. With a pastry brush, spread the 8 tablespoons of softened butter evenly over its entire outside surface.

Place the bird on its side on a rack set in a large, shallow roasting pan and roast it in the middle of the oven for 15 minutes. Turn it on its other side and roast 15 minutes longer. Then reduce the oven temperature to 325°, place the turkey breast side down and roast for 1 hour. Now turn it breast side up and roast it for about 1 hour longer, basting it every 15 minutes or so with the juices that have accumulated in the bottom of the pan.

To test for doneness, pierce the thigh of the turkey with the tip of a small, sharp knife. The juice that trickles out should be a clear yellow; if it is slightly pink, return the bird to the oven and roast for another 5 to 10 minutes. Transfer it to a heated platter and let it rest for 10 minutes or so for easier carving.

Meanwhile, skim off and discard all but a thin film of fat from the roasting pan. Stir the flour into the fat and cook over moderate heat for 2 to 3 minutes, meanwhile scraping in the brown particles clinging to the bottom and sides of the pan.

Pour in the reserved turkey stock (first skimming it of all surface fat) and, stirring constantly with a wire whisk, cook over high heat until the sauce comes to a boil, thickens and is smooth. Reduce the heat to low and simmer uncovered for about 5 minutes, then strain the gravy through a fine sieve into a serving bowl or sauceboat. Taste for seasoning and stir in the reserved chopped liver. Carve the turkey at the table, following the directions on page 28, and present the gravy separately.

Creamed Onions

To serve 8

To peel the onions, drop them into boiling water and let them boil briskly for about 30 seconds. Drain the onions in a sieve or colander under cold running water and cut off the root ends with a small, sharp knife. Slip off the papery outer skin of each onion and trim the top neatly.

Drop the onions into enough lightly salted boiling water to barely cover them. Reduce the heat to its lowest setting, partially cover the pan and simmer the onions for about 20 minutes, or until they show only slight resistance when pierced with the point of a small, sharp knife. Drain the onions in a sieve set over a bowl and set them aside. Measure and reserve 1 cup of the cooking liquid.

In a heavy 3- to 4-quart saucepan, melt the butter over moderate heat. When the foam begins to subside, add the flour and mix well. Stirring constantly with a wire whisk, pour in the reserved cup of cooking liquid, the milk and cream and cook over high heat until the sauce comes to a boil, thickens lightly and is smooth.

Reduce the heat to low and simmer the sauce for 3 or 4 minutes. Then stir in the nutmeg, salt and white pepper and taste for further seasoning. Add the onions and, turning them about gently with a spoon from time to time, simmer for a few minutes longer until they are heated through. Serve at once from a heated bowl.

2½ pounds small white onions
4 tablespoons butter
4 tablespoons flour
1½ cups milk
½ cup heavy cream
¼ teaspoon ground nutmeg, preferably freshly grated
1 teaspoon salt
Ground white pepper

Roast turkey, packed with savory oyster stuffing, is presented with rich pan gravy, cranberry-orange relish and creamed onions.

II

Three Crops from the Indians

Quite a lot of old-time New England cooking was based on the three native crops—corn, squash and beans—that anthropologists call "the Indian triad." Of the three, corn was king. The colonists were delighted with the way it thrived in almost any soil and gave much bigger yields than the wheat and rye they brought from the old country. But for their women it was a problem. The flour ground from corn looked much like wheat flour. It smelled good, and they knew it was nutritious, but it stubbornly resisted their efforts to make it into anything like the wheat or rye bread that their menfolk were used to.

Their breadmaking method was, of course, the ancient (and, alas, now largely neglected) art of mixing flour and water and kneading them with a little yeast into a smooth dough. When this is left to itself for a few hours in a warm place, the living yeast cells grow and give off carbon dioxide gas that fills the dough with bubbles and makes it swell. The bubbles expand in the heat when the raised dough is baked and are then made permanent by the thin but stiffening walls of dough around them. The result is a tender, digestible food not at all like the dough it was made from.

Such leavened bread had long been the staple of Europeans, but few 17th Century Englishwomen knew that making it depends on a peculiar property of wheat and its near relatives. These grains contain gluten, a sticky protein material that holds the dough in an elastic mass that retains the gas bubbles. Not so with corn. It must have been a sad occasion when the Pilgrim women first discovered that dough made of corn flour, which is poor in gluten and hence cannot hold the bubbles, refuses to rise.

The Indians' corn found its way into all manner of colonial food. Nowhere does it appeal more than in corn chowder, the ingredients for which are shown here. Like all New England chowders, the corn version includes potatoes, onions, salt pork and milk, cream or both.

Three kinds of beans that are widely used in New England cooking are *(from top)* Great Northern beans, pea beans and cranberry beans. The latter is one of hundreds of varieties of horticultural shell beans grown in Vermont, New Hampshire and Maine. The shell beans are not widely available in dried form, but pink or pinto beans may be substituted in recipes and will give similar color and flavor.

To find out what happened when they tried to make bread of corn flour in the traditional European manner, I ran an experiment. First I mixed ordinary bread dough, using the simplest possible recipe: just wheat flour, water, yeast and salt. I kneaded it properly and set it aside in a warm place to rise. Then I did the same again, substituting finely ground corn meal for the wheat flour. The same amount of water that I had used for the wheat dough made the corn meal somewhat moist, but it remained crumbly when I tried to knead it. I had to add more water to make it form a dough that barely held together.

After a few hours the wheat dough rose dutifully to twice its original size. The corn dough did nothing; it had a slightly sour, carbon-dioxide smell that proved the yeast was working, but it did not rise at all. I baked both loaves. The wheat loaf swelled up, browned nicely and tasted fine. It was not the best bread ever baked, but like all fresh homemade bread it was better than anything made in a commercial bakery. The corn loaf, baking right beside it in the oven, hardly changed appearance. It did not swell up; it did not brown. It got hard and brittle on the outside, but when I tried to slice it with a bread knife, it fell apart in moist, sour crumbs. Apparently the gas generated by the yeast had escaped at once. It formed no bubbles, and it left the corn particles in such a condition that they did not stick together. It would have taken an unusually hungry Pilgrim to down my leavened corn bread.

I am sure that ancient custom died hard, that over and over again the settlers' wives tried to make leavened bread out of yeast and corn flour. It never worked, and in a sense this was a blessing. They were determined to utilize their cheap and plentiful corn, and some of the things they learned to make out of it after their original setback are among the pleasantest items of New England cookery.

One of the rules the early housewives learned by sad experience is that corn meal cooperates if you do *not* try to form it into thick, European-style loaves. This is the principle the civilized Indians of Mexico followed when they made their thin corn tortillas. The backwoods New England Indians did not make tortillas, and probably never heard of them. If they had, the English settlers probably would have copied the technique, and tortillas might be as popular in modern Boston as they are in Mexico.

The New England equivalent of the tortilla, though no one thinks of it that way, is jonnycake (also known as johnnycake). The simplest recipes call for nothing but corn meal, hot water and a little salt. The water must be actually boiling hot. If it is not, it cannot dissolve starch and the corn meal will not hold together well. The batter should be fairly thin, but not as thin as wheat-cake batter. When dumped by large spoonfuls onto a hot, lightly greased griddle, it should spread out so it is not more than a quarter of an inch thick. When the cakes have browned underneath —which takes longer than for wheat pancakes—they can be turned over for brief browning on top, or can be put in the oven for finishing. They are not at all like wheat cakes: even when made with nothing but corn meal, water and salt, they are crisp on the outside, soft inside, and delicious, especially when eaten with butter and molasses or maple syrup.

Jonnycake dates from perhaps 1621, when the first Pilgrim woman desperately poured corn batter on a hot griddle, and like most eatables of re-spectable age it has evolved innumerable versions. Some authorities insist that the corn meal be heated in the oven before mixing so it will not cool the water too quickly. Others think such niceties unnecessary. A small amount of sugar is often added to the mix, and some cooks use milk, cream, butter, chopped suet, pork cracklings, baking powder or molasses. All these variations are worth trying, and jonnycake can be baked as well as fried. In Vermont it is customary to pour melted butter over the batter before baking it in a very hot oven.

The most famous variety is Rhode Island jonnycake, which Rhode Is-landers take so seriously that they hold contests to crown the mighty man who can eat the most of it. Traditionally it is supposed to be made only in Rhode Island from especially fine white locally grown corn that is water ground—meaning ground between millstones turned by a water wheel. My personal favorite is baked jonnycake mixed or anointed with plenty of butter, but I like fried jonnycake too, and I confess to the heretical belief that commercial corn meal, yellow or white, makes just as good jonnycake as fancy water-ground meal.

Another simple corn dish—nothing could be simpler—is corn mush, the hasty pudding of the colonists. Probably every corn-growing people makes mush by heating or boiling corn meal with water. Polenta, the staple food of Italian peasants, is corn mush, and so is the mealie porridge of many Africans. The New Englanders learned to make mush from the In-dians; they ate it in great quantities, as some still do. But they also used it as an approach to two dishes that are much better than plain mush.

The first of these, fried mush, was not hard to invent. When corn meal is boiled with water the resulting mush remains liquid only as long as it is warm. When it cools it solidifies to a springy solid that does not melt when heated again. Every early New England housewife must have no-ticed this behavior the first time she made too much hasty pudding for her family to eat immediately. The hardened mush defied warming over in the pot, and since she was a saving soul like most New Englanders, she did not want to waste it. So she tried cutting it in slices that she heated with lard in a frying pan.

Wonderful! Seldom does so simple a dish taste so good. Fried mush serves as a kind of pancake, but it has a flavor and texture all its own. When eaten with molasses or maple syrup, it does not soak up these pleas-ant additives; it keeps them on the outside where they can be tasted to the full. When I was a boy my mother kept blocks of solidified mush in the icebox and fried half-inch slices for me whenever I declared at breakfast that I was good and hungry. Nothing could be easier to prepare, and as many New Englanders noted approvingly, nothing could be cheaper.

The second mush-based corn dish, Indian pudding (Recipe Index), is more elaborate. It was not originated by the Indians as its name seems to imply; they lacked most of its ingredients. Its name comes from the fact that the colonists called corn "Indian corn" to distinguish it from wheat, which they called simply corn as the British do. Corn meal they called "In-dian" or sometimes "Injun."

Indian (or Injun) pudding is essentially milk flavored with molasses

Continued on page 40

Having soaked pea beans overnight, Mrs. Walker boils them until the skins burst when blown on *(below)*. She ladles them into an earthenware pot before adding the other ingredients *(above)*.

An Old Family Recipe for Boston Baked Beans

Since virtually every New England housewife has her own favorite way with Boston baked beans, the variety of authentic recipes is endless. Some flavor the pot with an onion buried in the beans before baking. Others add brown sugar, whole cloves, ginger or bay leaf. Some Cape Cod cooks even add half a cup of cream for the last hour of cooking. On these pages Mrs. Norman Walker, a Bostonian from an old New England family, demonstrates her own preferred method. The recipe is from her grandmother's time, when the family had baked beans with codfish cakes and green tomato relish on Sunday mornings.

Next a whole peeled onion is pressed into the beans, until it is just covered. Some cooks prefer to place the onion near the bottom of the pot, which gives the beans less of an onion flavor.

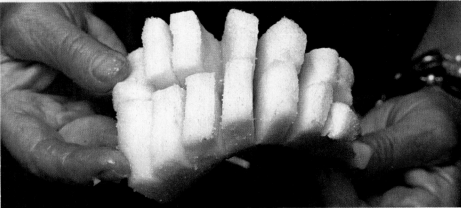

By scoring the salt pork, and then splaying it out, Mrs. Walker increases the surface area of the pork, so it will give off more of its flavor during the long hours of cooking.

Over the beans and pork, Mrs. Walker pours a mixture of molasses, brown sugar, salt, pepper and dry mustard. She adds boiling water to cover the contents, seals the pot, and bakes the beans in a 250° to 300° oven for at least 10 hours. During this time the pork fat melts slowly and permeates the beans.

and thickened with a little long-cooked corn meal, whose particles absorb the milk, swell up and acquire a softly granular texture. It can also contain eggs, sugar, butter, cinnamon or ginger. When properly baked it has a thin brown crust on top. It is served warm and semisolid and sometimes, nontraditionally, with ice cream on it. It tastes fine (corn and molasses seem to have a natural affinity) and since it is mostly milk, nothing could be better for filling the voids of hungry children. In its simpler forms it is extremely inexpensive.

Quite often in this book I shall cite the cheapness of a traditional New England dish, and I feel that it is in keeping for me to do so. The New Englanders were always a saving people. Their corner of the United States had few natural resources except a bracing climate and plenty of good harbors. They were forced to be economical, and often they managed to make a pleasure as well as a virtue of it. They especially guarded themselves from acquiring the illusion that expensive food is always the best. Often the opposite is the case, and New Englanders kept this welcome truth before their eyes. When a true Yankee samples a dish and decides after consideration that it is unusually good, he enjoys it even more if he can assure himself that it is cheap. I feel the same way, so I shall sometimes signal the reader when this Yankee appreciation is in order.

Corn bread is one of those cheap and excellent edibles. As soon as the colonists began to produce wheat, they found that several types of excellent bread can be made by mixing wheat (or rye) flour with corn meal, the function of the wheat flour being to contribute gluten to hold gas bubbles and make the bread reasonably light. One of the earliest of these discoveries was steamed Boston brown bread *(Recipe Index),* which is still a popular breadstuff today though the canned commercial version is not like the real thing.

There were many ways to make brown bread. If a family was poor or simply frugal, as so many of the New England pioneers were, they made brown bread mostly of cheap corn meal with just enough expensive wheat flour to keep it from being too solid and soggy, and it could be steamed in a pudding cloth in the family's single kettle if no proper tin was available. Extra-economical families were in the habit of saving stale bread, jonnycake, cookies, muffins or other baked goods, grinding them up with a little molasses and making "brown bread" of them. I suspect some of these adventitious mixtures were better than others.

The leavening bubbles that make brown bread rise when it is steamed come from baking soda, whose carbon dioxide is released by the lactic acid in sour milk, which most households do not have on hand because commercial pasteurized milk does not go sour gracefully; it rots. But commercial buttermilk does well enough; it is essentially sour milk whose cream has been removed to be sold separately. The molasses in brown bread contributes additional acid as well as flavor sweetness.

The brown-bread recipe my mother used had a character all its own. I remember watching the batter mixed and poured into a closed tin (sometimes a large baking-powder can) that stood upright on a trivet in a big covered kettle of simmering water. This routine was different from making other baked goods, so I paid attention. I remember the slight struggle

Opposite: The beans are baked uncovered for the last hour to crisp the pork—a delicacy that the head of the family traditionally reserves for himself. Pork sausages, frankfurters and beefsteak are all delicious with baked beans, but Mrs. Walker likes best of all a baked ham, glazed with brown sugar and studded with cloves. *(For another baked beans recipe, see page 30.)*

Baked beans are traditionally served in New England for Saturday dinner or Sunday breakfast—or both. But Mrs. Walker wanted to serve them at an early spring picnic on the terrace of her home in western Massachusetts. Most of the men of the family turned up to feast on beans, with green tomato relish, a ham, Boston brown bread, and a salad. Here Mrs. Walker pours out mugs of homemade cider for three of her grandchildren, while her son Bryce carves the ham and another son, Owen, dozes in the sun. When the eating was done, there was not a bean left in the pot.

to get the bread out of the tin several hours later when it had risen to fill the tin completely. The fragrant brown loaf was solid and firm with few holes, and moist but not at all soggy. It was tender and hard to slice when hot from the tin, but much more tractable a little later. It was only slightly sweet. I loved it, especially when it was toasted after sitting overnight, and I love it still. Brown bread is a real folk triumph.

Most modern brown breads, whether home-baked or bought in cans, are sweeter, lighter in texture, more crumbly and embellished with raisins. They are more like molasses-and-raisin cake. I prefer the old-fashioned kind for its fine, strong, simple flavor. Also it behaves better in the toaster. When cold it slices thin and does not break or crumble.

Many a New England recipe calls for molasses, as brown bread does, and there was an historical reason for this. In colonial times the sugar plantations in the West Indies used apparatus that could not extract the last bit of sucrose from cane juice. This remainder was sold as molasses for what it would bring. When Yankee traders sailed down to the islands with their boatloads of onions, salt fish and grain, they found plenty of molasses waiting for them that was hardly worth the cost of shipping it to Europe. They took barrels of it home, either to make rum or to sell as an inexpensive sweetener. It was cheaper than brown sugar, much cheaper than refined white sugar. New Englanders developed a taste for its flavor which they, and I, still have.

When I was a boy on Cape Cod, the local grocery kept by Sanford I.

Morse sold molasses by measure. There were two kinds: New Orleans, which was dark, and Porto (not Puerto) Rico, which was lighter. They were kept in big covered barrels with hand pumps on the lids. Mr. Morse first pumped the molasses into a very sticky quart measure and then poured it into the customer's container, usually a fruit jar or stone jug. Perhaps there were flies buzzing around this font of sweetness, but the young are not concerned about flies. I remember none.

What I do remember is that when the molasses in one of Mr. Morse's barrels got low, a fine time approached for the children of his favored customers. The molasses had stood in the barrel for a long time and had gradually deposited on the bottom an inch or so of whitish sugary sediment. Mr. Morse fed this to us with a long-handled spoon. It was wondrous smooth, like the silken ghost of sugar, and it had a gentle molasses taste I fear I shall never experience again.

Molasses-blessed brown bread is not, of course, strictly corn bread; it does not turn out well if it has more than half corn meal. But the colonists soon discovered another way to make corn bread thicker than jonnycake but still not soggy. The trick is to include a beaten egg, whose albumen holds the air beaten into it and also traps the gas given off by soda or baking powder. This makes the bread light and tender despite its corn meal content. Sugar and shortening may or may not be added, and the proportion of wheat flour increased. But for my taste corn bread is best without sugar and with less rather than more wheat flour.

No one seems to have had much better luck than the Pilgrims had with yeast-leavened corn bread. The nearest thing to it is Anadama bread *(Recipe Index)*, made with a little molasses and corn meal and a lot of flour. It is good but has hardly any corn flavor. The name is supposed to have come from a fisherman of Gloucester whose lazy wife, Anna, refused to bake bread. So he threw together a mixture of his own invention and named it "Anna, damn her." This is another derivation that I instinctively doubt, but Anadama bread is a reality; it is turned out by the millions of loaves at New England bread factories, and I have heard no better explanation for the name.

One of the nice things about corn is that its grains develop in fine, big, easily unzipped packages so they can be eaten, unlike wheat, when still immature. The Indians, both primitive and civilized, began eating their corn as soon as the kernels appeared and continued to eat it at all stages of ripeness up to harvest time. Modern Americans do this too, though one of the gastronomic tragedies of our urban civilization is that few people nowadays know how good young corn on the cob can be when it is really fresh. As soon as the ear is snapped off the stalk, bad things begin to happen to the milky kernels. Their natural sugar turns to tasteless starch; their delicate flavor fades. Young corn on the cob is still good after a two-day journey to the supermarket and another day of sitting on the vegetable tables there, but it is no longer the wonderful thing that it was in its recent innocence. Not all of us can grow corn in our backyards, but everyone, at least once in his life, should lay his hands on a dozen *freshly* picked ears (do not always believe what they tell you at the roadside stand) and rush them to the table, boiled, steamed or roasted, in less than two hours. Those who do this will know whereof I speak.

Young corn can be served in many pleasant ways besides on the cob. One way is in corn pancakes which are best made with kernels scraped or grated off the cob after each row has been slit open with a very sharp knife so the skins of the kernels are left behind. Use just enough batter to hold the corn together and cook it on a lightly greased griddle. Satisfactory corn pancakes can be made with frozen or canned corn kernels, but are not quite as good.

Perhaps the best dish of all made with young corn is corn chowder *(Recipe Index)*. Like all traditional dishes developed by the individualistic Yankee housewives, it has many versions. The essential ingredients are green corn kernels (preferably fresh or frozen though canned will do), milk or cream, potatoes, onions and fat salt pork. I note a modern prejudice against this last fine old material, and I attribute it to the commercial interests selling trade-named and highly advertised vegetable shortenings. These soulless chemicals have neither flavor, appearance nor texture, while salt pork contributes all three. It should be cut into small dice or shreds and fried until the bits are golden brown. Then the bits are removed and set aside while the sliced onions are delicately browned in the pork grease. The corn and the potatoes, diced or cut in small wedges, are added and boiled with just sufficient water until the potatoes are soft enough to contribute a little thickening. If more thickening is desired, add a little flour mixed with cold water. Remove from the heat, add the milk or cream and reheat but do not boil. Then sprinkle with the golden pork scraps. Your consumers will cheer.

I do not know, though I have tried to find out, whether the first settlers of New England were familiar with squash and with the variety of squash called pumpkin. After the Spanish conquest of Mexico in 1521 there had certainly been time for these big vegetables to spread from there, where they were developed as a crop, to parts of Europe where they grow equally well. So the Pilgrims may have had squash and pumpkin seeds of their own. On the other hand the word "squash" is of local Indian derivation (from *isquoutersquash*), which suggests that the settlers needed a name for a crop that was new to them. Whichever was the case, they ate a lot of squash and pumpkin, as told in a bit of 17th Century doggerel:

> *We have pumpkins at morning,*
> *Pumpkins at noon.*
> *If it were not for pumpkins*
> *We should be undoon.*

Pumpkins and the meaty winter squashes are nutritious, and they ripen early in a season when other fresh food is scarce, but plain boiled pumpkin or other squash is not tempting as a steady diet. The New Englanders, however, soon learned how to glorify squash, and they still eat more of it than most other Americans do. The most famous dish is pumpkin pie, which along with apple and mince pie was obligatory at the Thanksgiving dinner. Either pumpkin or squash can be used; some cooks prefer one, some the other. The recipes vary mostly in the spices used, which may include ginger, cinnamon, nutmeg and mace or allspice. A spectacular but nontraditional pumpkin pie *(Recipe Index)* calls for well-beaten egg whites folded in to give a puffy, chiffonlike texture.

I shall not concern myself with the crookneck summer squash, which I consider an insipid vegetable. My only willing contact with it as a child was to look for crookneck squashes that had been allowed to "go by" and had grown hard shells. By attaching stretched rubber bands I made them into guitars of a sort. The green and dark zucchini are better eating, and they are true squashes botanically, but they are recent imports, not part of the New England cuisine.

The ideal New England squash is the winter or Hubbard squash, with thick yellow or orange flesh. The shell may be of several colors and with or without lumps, and the shape varies all over the place. Some winter squashes have necks; other approach the pumpkin in shape. The acorn and turban squashes are winter squashes bred down in size to fit small families and to suit the convenience of supermarkets, which do not like to cut pieces of squash for customers as old-fashioned greengrocers did.

Good-quality winter squash is excellent baked. Chunks of it are sprinkled thinly with brown sugar and a little salt. A half-pat of butter is put in the shallow dishes formed by the curving upper sides of the squash, and the chunks are baked very slowly for several hours in a pan with a little water in it. This makes a good, not too plain vegetable. If a little ginger and cinnamon are added and more sugar and butter, baked squash becomes a party dish, much like squash pie with the squash's own shell doing the duty of the pie crust. Acorn and other small squashes cut in

Continued on page 50

The Odd Shapes and Rich Hues of New England's Squashes

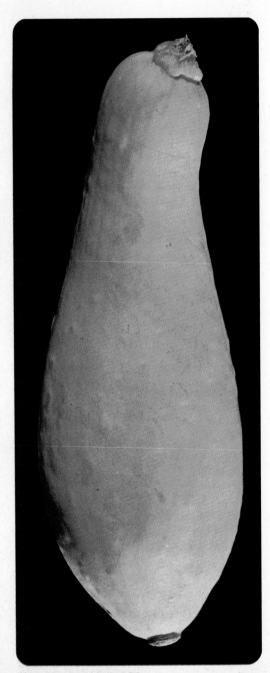

Summer Squashes

Despite their name, summer squashes are available the year around in most of the United States. They are picked well before full maturity, while still tender and relatively seedless. Soft-skinned and delicately flavored, they need be simply sliced and steamed.

YELLOW STRAIGHTNECK
Like all summer squashes, the straightneck is at its best when small, five to seven inches long.

WHITE PATTYPAN
Only about four to five inches across, this is the bantamweight of New England's varieties of squash. It turns from pale green to white as it ripens.

Winter Squashes

Harvested in late autumn (but
available all year in some areas),
winter squashes have hard,
sometimes gnarled skins that keep
the flesh moist for months, a virtue
the early settlers recognized by
storing them for the lean seasons.
These squashes have seeds that must
be discarded before cooking.

BLUE HUBBARD
This giant squash can weigh up to
14 pounds and grow to more than
18 inches long. Its thick, rough skin
belies the succulent orange flesh
within. Outside of New England,
the Hubbard is often sold already
cut up into convenient chunks.

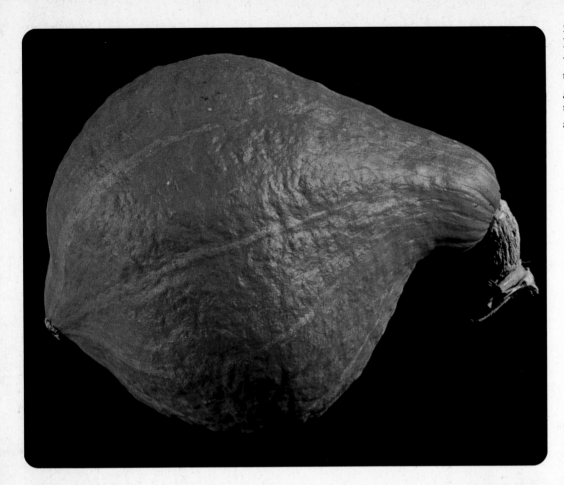

BOSTON MARROW
Probably the oldest known variety of winter squash in use today, the marrow grows a foot long, weighs up to 12 pounds, and has a distinctive tapered stem.

BUTTERNUT
A particular kitchen favorite, this abundant variety of squash, about nine inches long, is easily identifiable by its thick neck and light tan color.

TURK'S TURBAN
The bizarre shell of this small squash doubles as a serving dish for its own mashed or puréed pulp.

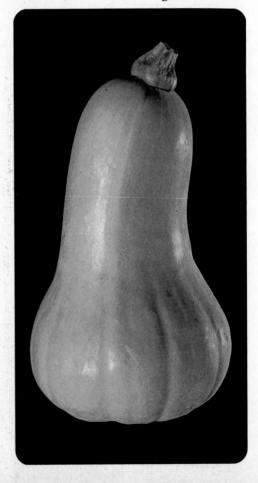

SUGAR PUMPKIN
The most celebrated of all squashes is the pumpkin. Millions are gouged out each year to make Halloween lanterns or are baked in Thanksgiving pies. This small, sweet variety, about eight inches in diameter, brightens roadside stands every fall.

ACORN
Popular with home gardeners, this grapefruit-sized squash has meaty, orange-yellow flesh that is especially suitable for baked dishes. The shell is sometimes marked with bright orange patches.

BUTTERCUP
The flavorful flesh of this small squash (about four and a half inches across) makes it a New England standby.

half can be baked this way and served as individual "casseroles," but their flesh is thinner and usually not as good.

Mashed squash improved with butter, sugar, molasses or other additives is not peculiar to New England, though I think it is served more often there. But a very New England trick is to add a little cooked and strained squash or pumpkin to cake, biscuit or pancake mixtures and rolls *(Recipe Index)*. It gives a distinctive flavor and a nice, moist texture.

It is hard to tell whether the first settlers had seen or heard of beans before reaching New England. All the familiar kinds of beans except broad beans and soy beans had originated in the New World and had had plenty of time to reach northern Europe before the Pilgrims set sail. But even if they knew about them, it looks as if the Pilgrims brought no beans of their own for seed; they were grateful for the baskets of many-colored beans that they found in an Indian cache on Cape Cod.

Ever since then, beans have been important in New England culinary affairs. In spite of their origin in Mexico, they grow perfectly well in New England's harsher climate. In no time the settlers sorted out the Indians' helter-skelter mixture into many standard types, large or small, red, white, yellow-eyed or speckled, and soon they developed a number of pleasant ways of cooking them.

Succotash the settlers took over directly from the Indians, who had created this excellent dish by their custom of putting everything they had into a single pot to boil. Ofen they had corn and beans, with or without meat. The settlers called the combination succotash, though the related Indian word seems to have meant hulled corn, and they developed the dish in two directions. One emphasized the meat and led to the ceremonial Plymouth succotash *(Recipe Index)* described in Chapter 1. The other became a sort of chowder that is not at all like the plain mixture of corn and beans that is now bought frozen or in cans as succotash. When made in the proper way, this succotash contains milk, butter, a trace of sugar and sometimes bits of browned salt pork. It is best when the corn is freshly scraped off the cob and the beans are shell beans; that is, fully grown but not yet dried. However, canned or frozen corn and dried beans, including lima beans, make excellent succotash if the beans are not cooked so long that they burst.

Another bean dish famous in New England culinary history is the bean porridge of New Hampshire and Vermont. It was made of beans and corn meal cooked with stew meat or soup bones. When cold it set hard and could be carried in blocks to be heated up on journeys or at distant work places. Lumber camps made it in massive amounts and put it out to freeze. When the cook served bean porridge, the first implement he reached for was an axe.

The most important bean dish was, and is, Boston baked beans *(Recipe Index,* indexed under Harlow House baked beans), which acquired tremendous traditional, almost religious significance. I have found no direct evidence that the Indians baked beans, but indirect evidence suggests that they did. In a few woodsy sections of New England the custom still persists (more as a ceremony than anything else) of baking beans in a bean hole: a small hole in the ground lined with stones. A fire is built in

In Massachusetts, the squashes of autumn are used to make whimsical harvest figures. This father-and-son pair, enthroned on a roadside in the central part of the state, have bodies made out of pumpkins, and arms and legs made of convincingly shaped butternut squashes.

the hole to heat the stones; then a covered pot of beans is put in and the hole is sealed with a flat stone or with branches and sod. This archaic way of cooking, which is much more trouble than it is worth, sounds Indian. It is obviously related to the clambake that the settlers adopted with such enthusiasm. Whether Indian or not, baked beans took hold quickly and were further improved when salt pork and molasses could be added.

Baked beans would have won popularity on their own, for they are a culinary triumph, but in early New England they got an additional boost from the fearsome Puritan Sabbath. My own immediate family was Unitarian and not strict about the Lord's Day, but a little farther back in my family history the Sabbath glowered like a thundercloud. My mother's mother remembered it as a doom of silence, stilling the laughter of children, and even, so it seemed, the songs of birds.

The dread day began at sundown on Saturday, an adaptation of Old Testament custom. My grandmother's family were Connecticut people who lived in a house that looked across a wide valley to distant hills in the west. On Saturday as the sun sank down toward those hills, the children gathered in front of the house, running, laughing, screaming as loudly as possible but keeping an eye on the setting sun. On the front porch sat Grandmother, rocking watchfully in her rocking chair. When the sun touched the horizon, and she stopped rocking, the children's yells and screams rose to a desperate pitch. When the last spark of the sun had disappeared, Grandmother stood up grimly. Utter silence fell; the Sabbath was on the land.

On Sunday the play was repeated in reverse: in silence the children watched the sun go down, and Grandmother stood in front of her rocking chair. When the last of the sun was gone, she sat down with a beaming smile. The children screamed their heads off. The Lord's Day was over.

Baked beans played an important role in this weekly ritual. On the Sabbath no work was supposed to be done; some strict families even tied up the kitchen pump to head off Sabbathbreaking. There were exceptions to this rule; fires had to be stoked in winter to keep all hands from freezing, but cooking was forbidden. So on Saturday morning or even on Friday night a tremendous charge of beans was started on its long passage through the great brick oven. The first big pot was eaten piping hot, along with brown bread, on Saturday night when the Sabbath was already in full force. Serving it was not considered forbidden work. The remains were left in the oven where they kept plenty warm for Sunday breakfast. They were acceptably warm even when the family returned from church. So baked beans enabled the strictest Sabbatarians to soften the rigors of the Lord's Day.

In most families the Puritan Sabbath died out in the 19th Century, and enormous freshly cooked Sunday dinners were permitted, but baked beans and brown bread kept their popularity as the traditional Saturday night dish. They also acquired another ritual function; to serve as the *pièce* of church bean suppers. Every now and then, and in some towns pretty often, the ladies of the church got together to present their best beans at long, sociable tables in the church basement. Each lady had her own ideas, and the variety offered was astonishing, for each of them baked a different kind of bean with different flavoring and treatment. I remember my father, a bean lover though not a steady church attendant, going early to suppers in the Unitarian church so he could be sure of getting some of a certain lady's beans. Besides the conventional brown bread, the ladies often contributed cakes to delight their neighbors and demonstrate their cooking skill. My father told me of one occasion when an elderly farmer came early, sat down and with studied inattention ate slice after slice of golden sponge cake. "Best bread I ever et," he said.

There are no bean suppers in my Cape Cod town now except the rather commercial affairs run by the lady Masons in summer and attended by dense crowds of summer people; the beans served there in almost carload lots are necessarily below the oldtime standard. But beans are still baked in our town in many different ways; my sister collected a dozen distinct recipes with no trouble at all. Some households prefer yellow-eyed beans; others use white pea beans or red kidney beans. Actually any kind of bean can be baked, including southern black-eyed peas (which are really beans) and small red cow peas, which are also beans. Real peas will not do, whether split or unsplit, green or yellow; they come apart too readily.

Nearly every New England cook has her own ideas about the secondary ingredients. Salt pork is obligatory, and its rind is always scored in squares, but some women bury it in the beans, others stick it on top so the rind will brown. Molasses is always used, but the amount varies widely, and sometimes sugar (white or brown) is substituted for part of it. Some cooks insist on using mustard, others do not. Some put an onion at the bottom of the pot; others decry the practice. Tomato is seldom if ever cooked with New England baked beans.

The baking time advocated varies from a few hours up to all day in a very slow oven. The longer the better is my belief. The beans do not disintegrate, but during this wealth of baking time something wonderful happens to their flavor, which multiplies and diversifies. The bean pot is covered to keep too much steam from escaping, and water is added when the surface of the liquid sinks to bean level. An hour or so before the beans are to be served, the cover is taken off, allowing the top layer of beans to dry slightly and form a delectable crust. The squares of pork rind, which by this time are soft and edible, turn a toothsome brown. The final product is a fragrant delight, a dish for any king. There is nothing better for a hungry man, woman or child than a perfectly baked pot of Boston baked beans.

I feel I should now, Yankee-like, signal the cheapness of this excellent dish, which will feed a whole family at almost negligible cost. When I was still a child, though a large one, I used to go with my friend George Wing to the Unitarian bean suppers. The price was 25 cents per person, and at one time our agreed objective was to eat so much that the church would lose money on us. We ate and ate, first eagerly, then with effort, then with pain, until we felt pressure behind our eyeballs and were too torpid to play the games, such as "going to Jerusalem," that came after supper. We felt we had won our contest with the church, but when I boasted about this to my father, he did a calculation and shook his head. "No," he said. "The church made at least 10 cents on each of you." Bean suppers are still cheap, but so are beans. I am sure the church still makes modest money on the most gluttonous child.

New England's breads are as varied as its vistas. Parker House rolls *(top left)* were devised at the Boston hotel of that name; Portuguese sweet bread, next to the rolls, is a legacy of fishermen who crossed the Atlantic to fill their holds in New England waters. Squash flavors the Mayo Farm's rolls *(above)*; corn meal and molasses give Anadama bread at bottom left its crunch and color.

To make 8 five-inch-round cakes

1 cup white corn meal
1 teaspoon salt
1 tablespoon butter, softened, plus
    ¼ cup butter, melted, plus 4
    butter pats
1 cup boiling water
¼ to ½ cup milk
Maple syrup

Rhode Island Jonnycake

Combine the corn meal, salt and softened butter in a deep bowl. Stirring constantly, pour in the water in a thin stream. When the butter melts and the liquid is absorbed, add ¼ cup of milk. Beat until the batter holds its shape lightly in the spoon. If necessary, add more milk by the teaspoonful.

Heat a large griddle or heavy skillet over moderate heat until a drop of water flicked onto it splutters instantly. Brush the griddle or skillet lightly with melted butter. To form each cake, ladle ¼ cup of the batter into the pan. Cook 1 or 2 cakes at a time, leaving enough space so that they can spread into 5-inch rounds. Fry them for 3 minutes on each side, or until they are golden and crisp around the edges. As they brown, transfer the jonnycakes to a heated plate and drape with foil to keep them warm while you cook the rest, brushing the pan with melted butter as necessary. If the batter thickens, thin it with another tablespoon of milk.

Top each cake with half a butter pat and some syrup, and serve at once.

To make about 2 dozen doughnuts
    and 4 to 5 dozen doughnut balls

1 cup buttermilk
½ cup dark molasses
2 tablespoons lard, melted and
    cooled
4½ to 5½ cups flour
1 tablespoon baking soda
1 teaspoon ground ginger
1 teaspoon ground cinnamon
1 teaspoon ground nutmeg
2 eggs
2 cups sugar
Vegetable oil for deep frying

Molasses Doughnuts

Pour the buttermilk, molasses and lard into a bowl and mix well. Combine 4½ cups of the flour, the baking soda, ginger, cinnamon and nutmeg and sift them onto a plate. Set both mixtures aside.

In a deep bowl, beat the eggs and 1 cup of the sugar with a wire whisk or a rotary or electric beater for 4 or 5 minutes, or until the mixture falls in a slowly dissolving ribbon from the beater when it is lifted from the bowl. Beat in the buttermilk mixture. Then add the sifted dry ingredients about ½ cup at a time, beating well after each addition. Cover the bowl with wax paper and refrigerate for at least 30 minutes.

Line one or two large baking sheets with wax paper. Cut off about ¼ of the dough and place it on a lightly floured surface. Brush a rolling pin with flour and roll the dough out about ⅓ inch thick. If the dough sticks, dust a little flour over and under it. With a 2¾-inch doughnut cutter, cut out as many doughnuts as you can and, using a wide metal spatula, transfer them to the paper-lined pans. Refrigerate until ready to fry. Break off another ¼ of the dough, roll it out, cut out more doughnuts and refrigerate as before. Repeat until all the dough has been used, but do not reroll the scraps or the doughnuts made from them may be tough. Instead use a 1-inch cutter to form balls out of the scraps.

Pour oil into a deep fryer or large, heavy saucepan to a depth of 3 inches and heat it to a temperature of 360° on a deep-frying thermometer. At the same time place ½ cup of sugar in a paper bag and set it aside.

Deep-fry the doughnuts 4 or 5 at a time, turning them with a slotted spoon for 3 minutes, or until they are puffed and brown. Drain the doughnuts briefly on paper towels, then drop 2 at a time into the bag and shake to coat them with sugar. (Add sugar to the bag as needed.) Place the doughnuts on a platter to cool while you fry and sugar the rest.

Yankee breakfasts fortify the body for a day's work. On the table here, Canadian bacon and fried eggs are bolstered by molasses doughnuts *(left)*, Rhode Island jonnycakes *(right)* and hasty pudding *(top)*.

Corn-and-bean succotashes range from the meaty Plymouth type to all-vegetable ones for winter *(top)* and summer *(right)*.

To serve 4

1 cup (½ pound) dried
   horticultural shell beans such as
   cranberry beans, or substitute
   dried pink or pinto beans
1 medium-sized onion, peeled and
   pierced with 2 whole cloves
4 sprigs fresh parsley and 1 small
   bay leaf tied together with
   kitchen string
1 tablespoon plus 1 teaspoon salt
2 cups fresh corn kernels, cut from
   about 4 large ears of corn, or
   substitute 2 cups frozen corn
   kernels, thoroughly defrosted
½ cup heavy cream
4 tablespoons butter, cut into
   ½-inch bits
Freshly ground black pepper

Winter Succotash

In a heavy 2- to 3-quart saucepan, bring 1 quart of water to a boil over high heat. Drop in the dried beans and boil them briskly uncovered for about 2 minutes. (The water should cover the beans by at least 2 inches; if necessary, add more.)

Turn off the heat and let the beans soak for 1 hour. Then add the onion, the parsley-and-bay leaf bouquet and 1 tablespoon of salt. Bring to a boil again, stirring until the salt dissolves.

Reduce the heat to low, partially cover the pan, and simmer for about 1 hour, or until the beans are tender. Check the beans from time to time and add more boiling water if needed. Drain the beans through a fine sieve, discarding the cooking liquid. Then pick out and discard the onion and the parsley and bay leaf.

Return the beans to the saucepan and add the corn and cream. Stirring from time to time, bring to a boil over moderate heat, reduce the heat to low and cook for 2 or 3 minutes until the liquid in the pan has thickened slightly and the corn is tender and hot.

Add the butter, the remaining teaspoon of salt and a few grindings of pepper and continue to stir until the butter melts. Taste for seasoning and serve at once from a heated bowl.

58

Mayo Farm's Squash Rolls

To make about 30 rolls

½ pound acorn, Hubbard or
  butternut squash, peeled, seeded
  and cut into 2-inch chunks
½ cup lukewarm water (110° to
  115°)
2 packages active dry yeast
½ cup sugar
5 to 6 cups flour
1 teaspoon salt
1 cup lukewarm milk (110° to
  115°)
½ cup plus 4 teaspoons butter,
  softened, plus 2 tablespoons
  butter, melted

Pour water into the lower part of a steamer to within about 1 inch of the top pan. Bring the water to a boil, put the squash in the top pan and set it in place. Immediately cover the pan and steam over high heat for 30 minutes, or until the squash is tender.

(Lacking a steamer, you can improvise one by using a large pot equipped with a tightly-fitting cover, and a standing colander or a collapsible steaming basket on legs. Pour water into the pot to within about 1 inch of the perforated container and bring it to a boil. Place the squash in the basket or colander, set it in place, and cover the pot. Steam over high heat for about 30 minutes, or until the squash is soft.)

Purée the squash through a food mill or mash it smoothly with a fork and set it aside. (There should be about ½ cup of purée.)

Pour the ½ cup of lukewarm water into a small bowl and add the yeast and a pinch of the sugar. Let the yeast and sugar rest for 2 or 3 minutes, then mix well. Set in a warm, draft-free place (such as an unlighted oven) for about 10 minutes, or until the yeast bubbles up and the mixture almost doubles in volume.

Combine 5 cups of the flour, the remaining sugar and the salt, sift them together into a deep mixing bowl and make a well in the center. Pour in the yeast mixture, add the squash purée, the milk and ½ cup of softened butter and, with a large wooden spoon, gradually beat the dry ingredients into the liquid ones. Continue to beat until the dough is smooth and can be gathered into a compact ball.

Place the ball on a lightly floured surface and knead, pushing the dough down with the heels of your hands, pressing it forward and folding it back on itself. As you knead, incorporate up to 1 cup more flour, sprinkling it over the ball by the tablespoonful until the dough is no longer moist and sticky. Then continue to knead for about 10 minutes, or until the dough is smooth, shiny and elastic.

With a pastry brush, spread 2 teaspoons of the softened butter evenly over the inside of a large bowl. Set the dough in the bowl and turn it about to butter the entire surface of the dough. Drape the bowl with a kitchen towel and put it in the draft-free place for about 1 hour to allow the dough to double in volume.

Brush the remaining 2 teaspoons of softened butter over the bottom and sides of two 9-inch cake pans. Punch the dough down with a single blow of your fist and, on a lightly floured surface, roll it out into a rough rectangle about 1 inch thick.

With a cookie cutter or the rim of a glass, cut the dough into 2½-inch rounds. Gather the scraps into a ball, roll them out as before and cut out as many more 2½-inch rounds as you can. With the blunt edge of a table knife, make a deep crease just off-center in each round, taking care not to cut all the way through. Fold the smaller part of the round over the larger part and press the edges together securely.

Arrange the rolls about ½ inch apart in the buttered cake pans and brush the tops with the melted butter. Set the rolls in the draft-free place to rise for about 15 minutes.

Meanwhile preheat the oven to 450°. Bake the rolls in the middle of the oven for 12 to 15 minutes, or until golden brown. Serve the rolls hot.

III

"The Aboundance of Sea Fish"

At 6 a.m. on the Boston Fish Pier, Jack Dinn rigs a boom to unload a trawler just in with its catch. He is a "lumper," who transfers fish from boat to pier, and like many men in his trade, used to be a fisherman himself in the 400-boat fleet based in Boston.

In 1629 Francis Higginson, a Puritan minister of Salem in the Massachusetts Bay Colony, dispatched an enthusiastic letter to a friend in England. "The aboundance of sea fish," he wrote, "are almost beyond believing, and sure I should scarse have believed it, except I had seen it with my own eyes. I saw great store of whales and crampusse [grampus, or blackfish] and such aboundance of mackerils that it would astonish one to behold, likewise cod-fish in abundance on the coast, and in their season are plentifully taken. There is a fish called a basse, a most sweet and wholesome fish as ever I did eat, it is altogether as good as our fresh sammon. . . . Of this fish our fishers take many hundreds together, which I have seen lying on the shore to my admiration. . . . And besides basse we take plenty of scate and thornbacks, and aboundance of lobsters and the least boy in the plantation may catch and eat what he will of them. . . . And here is aboundance of herring, turbut, sturgion, cuskes, hadocks, mullets, eeles, crabbes, muscles, and oysters."

Not all these delicacies, let alone the whales, are as plentiful as when Higginson wrote. Except in Maine and Canada the salmon are gone; they could not cope with power dams built across rivers. Sturgeon are few, and shad are far less plentiful than they used to be. Their monument is the shadbush that flecks brushy lowlands with mounds of white to signal the time in spring when the shad once crowded into the rivers. But the alewives—the bony herring with which the Indians taught the Pilgrims to fertilize their corn—still run up the smaller streams in enormous numbers, and their roe is delicious when broiled, as good as shad roe. (They are not to be confused with the smaller, land-locked alewives of the Northern Great Lakes.) If you find any New England alewives offered for sale, do not pass them up. Their run is a sign of spring in many streams of the region, and crowds of nature-starved urbanites gather to watch them struggle up the fish-ladders to ponds where they spawn.

Most ocean fish have not yet been affected by industrialization. For reasons having to do with ocean ecology they are still abundant. The cold sea water carried south to New England from arctic Davis Strait by the Labrador Current is naturally fertile. Even far from sources of pollution it is slightly turbid and green, not blue, which means that it swarms with minute organisms, the grass of the sea, that are the support of most marine life. As a born-and-bred New Englander, I was almost painfully surprised when I first went out as far as the Gulf Stream and saw the ship's bow-wave curling bright blue. To me it looked unnatural, like bluing in a wash tub, and somehow shocking. Perhaps I realized instinctively that clear blue tropical water is comparatively free of these tiny food sources.

The sea water of New England and of Canada's Maritime Provinces is anything but sterile; the plankton that make it green support a marvelous living spectrum. Every rocky pool is furred with seaweed and barnacles and scuttling with tiny creatures. Mudflats are full of the holes of clams and sea-worms. Even wave-beaten beaches jump with shrimplike sand fleas with blue, crossed eyes. In deeper water swim the fish, as serene and voracious as ever. On the bottom flatfish snuggle into the sand waiting in ambush for prey. Above them cruise the haddock and cod browsing on crabs, worms and mollusks with their downward-turning mouths. Fierce pollock patrol the midwaters catching what they can. On the surface vast schools of herring and mackerel move majestically up the coast pursued by ferocious tuna, swift as torpedoes. Schools of sporty striped bass chase after schools of squid, those strange jet-propelled mollusks that swim with the agility of fish. There are bluefish and swordfish, puff-fish and sculpins, weakfish and tautog, sharks, skates and rays, and angler fish that lie on the bottom and decoy gullible victims with edible-looking lures suspended above their mouths.

In spite of this continued plenty, the weekend anglers who swarm down to the shore usually catch very little. This is mostly their own fault, due to their heroic image of themselves. Once I took my son, then about six years old, to the mouth of the Cape Cod ship canal where we found perhaps 100 people, including very old ladies, vigorously fishing off a bulkhead. They were casting out into the canal, using expensive gear and large hooks baited with hunks of real or imitation squid. They were hoping to catch striped bass, but I knew no bass had been caught, seen or felt there for a considerable time.

I had a better idea. Since my purpose was to please my son, not to catch bass where none existed, I had brought a simple hand line armed with a very small hook. I baited the hook with a tidbit out of a can of chopped clams and showed my son how to drop it vertically off the bulkhead. Almost at once he got a bite and with cries of joy hauled up a fish about seven inches long, a young pollock some of whose ancestors I had caught off that same bulkhead 30 years before. A few minutes later he caught another, and then another. In an hour we had a pail half full, mostly infant pollock which, though small, make excellent eating. We took them home and cooked them within half an hour. Pan-fried with a little butter and chopped chives, they were sweet and delicate.

While we were hauling them in at the bulkhead, we got glares from the bass fishermen. Only the littlest children came to share my son's pleasure. The adults, who had not had a bite, were frustrated and furious. They thought of themselves as opponents of the great, fighting striped bass and nothing less. Even to please their children, they would not condescend to catch small pollock.

Striped-bass fishing is now a major enterprise in thickly settled southern New England. On fine days in summer every beach, pier and rocky headland has its bass-hunters, often crowds of them. Seldom do they catch anything at all. The bass, which swim in schools, are either absent or so full of squid, their favorite food, that the fishermen's offerings do not interest them. But once in a great while a hungry school comes close to shore, even occasionally into the Cape Cod Canal, and swallows any bait that looks faintly edible. Then dozens of great "stripers" are dragged out of the water, flapping mightily. Sometimes a single fisherman catches a carload or a boatload of them, just as people did in that far-off time of Francis Higginson.

Immediately something happens that Higginson knew not of. The lucky fishermen rush to the telephone to boast of their triumph, and the news flies far on electronic wings. Fishermen's hangouts hear it; radio stations broadcast it. Within a few hours cars and camper-trucks converge on the lucky spot, sometimes jamming the narrow roads. By this time the surviving bass are usually miles away, swimming determinedly in their endless hunt for squid.

Bass fishermen seem to get pleasure out of their long-odds hobby; perhaps the real attraction is an excuse to commune with sand and surf and sea. My own feeling toward fish is broader and less mystical: I like to eat them. Practically every fish that can be caught in the sea off New England and eastern Canada is good to eat. I have heard that some sharks are wholly inedible, but dogfish, which are small sharks, are not at all bad. They are commonly eaten in Europe. I have never tried angler fish because I have never seen a live or freshly caught one, only their ugly carcasses cast up on the beach after an onshore blow, but I hear they are edible too, as are the equally ugly sculpins and other trash fish.

So I urge readers to try anything, even the little miscellaneous fish they catch to entertain their children. The best way to prepare these small fish is to clean them but not split them apart. This makes it much easier to keep track of the bones. Just pan-fry them quickly, after rolling them in corn meal to keep the delicate skin from sticking to the pan. If the fish is excessively bony, as sculpins are, it is better to fry just the tail section where the meat is concentrated.

Some of the small species that can be caught with simple tackle right off our northeastern shores are among the world's best eating fish. The great schools of little mackerel and bluefish seem to break up in summer and come up to the beaches and into tidal inlets. They are searching for

Continued on page 66

One of the men at Plymouth Colony wrote in his diary: ". . . in April there is a fish much like a herring that comes up into the small brooks to spawn, and when the water is not knee deep they will presse up through your hands, yea, thow you beat at them with cudgels, and in such abundance as is incredible." Today *Pomolobus pseudoharengus,* a kind of herring also known as an alewife, still runs in from the sea each spring to spawn in fresh-water ponds. At Brewster, Massachusetts, a fish ladder has been built to help the alewives climb a steep section of Stoney Brook. In late April or early May the word goes around: "The herring are running." They come in so thickly the tumbling water of the stream is black with them, as they leap from pool to pool up toward Mill Pond. Men, women and children scramble to catch them *(left),* using nets or simply their bare hands. At right, a mother-and-son team have a flapping prize in their net. Most people eat only the roe and discard the rest of the alewife which is rather bony. The author explains in this chapter how to cope with the bone problem.

smaller prey, and will take any shiny, fishlike bait even though it is nothing but a strip of bright tin. Suddenly everyone in town is trying to give tinker mackerel to each other.

Tinker mackerel and bluefish weighing half a pound or so are divinely delicious eating. They are seldom offered in markets, apparently because the public does not know about them and so the demand is too small to encourage commercial fishermen to go after them. They should be lightly fried, whole in oil or butter, and need no seasoning but salt.

People brought up in seacoast towns appreciate small fish, often preferring them for their superior texture and flavor, but most inlanders and city people demand solid steaks or fillets cut from large fish. This is because they have undue respect for fish bones, which they fear will get stuck in their throats and cause them to choke. There is no good reason for this fear; the bones of nearly all fish are arranged in logical patterns and usually can be removed with ease. One exception is shad, which has lots of insidious bones in unexpected places.

A fish is built on a simple plan; it has a long, jointed backbone running from head to tail. Small bones extend up and down from the vertebrae giving support for the flesh. Toward the forward end of the fish the downward-pointing bones are curved, forming a rib-cage to contain the stomach and other inner works. If the fish has bony fins, as many do, they are often associated with small bones in the flesh.

When you are armed with this knowledge it is easy to eat any whole small fish without the slightest bone trouble. But do not slam into it with knife and fork as if it were a slice of ham. Approach it with circumspection, turning the flesh on one side away from the backbone and the small fin bones, if any. Watch out for the ribs, which sometimes come loose from the backbone, and for small bones connected with the swimming fins. Then turn the fish over and do the same on the other side. All this should take about 15 seconds. Only then should you start eating—in perfect peace of mind. After you have done this trick a couple of times you will be able to tell landbound ignoramuses that only small, bone-rich sea fish are really worth eating. You will certainly tell them that tinker mackerel are much better than brook trout, most of which were raised in state hatcheries on some unpleasant feed such as ground-up hog spleens and were caught a day or two after they were dumped in the streams.

Most fish sold commercially are caught by professional fishermen who know their business and go to the right places equipped with the right gear, which is not rod and reel. The kind of gear depends on the fish sought. Groundfish (those that live close to the bottom) are commercially taken on baited hooks attached by short lines to a long, heavier line that is sunk along the bottom and left there for several hours. When the fisherman picks up the bright-colored marker buoy and hauls up the line, he hopes to find great codfish on the hooks. Codfish are not vigorous; they make little attempt to escape, and when they are pulled to the surface they fight about as heroically as old auto tires.

Along the twisting coast from Connecticut to Labrador little boats putt-putt out in the morning with lines carefully coiled in tubs, and putt-putt back with their catch before sundown. Fish caught in this way have the highest quality. They are alive and well when boated and are taken ashore in a few hours, put on ice and rushed by truck to market. Restaurants a thousand miles away can serve them on the day after they left the sea. That is, they can if they want to, and more and more restaurants and fish markets far from New England are getting fresh fish by air. So more and more inland Americans and Canadians are finding out what a really fresh sea fish can taste like.

The great bulk of bottom fish is caught by large powerful boats that go far out for a week or more with otter trawls. These are great bag-shaped nets dragged on or near the bottom behind the boat and held open by submerged otter boards that look like doors and are generally called doors. Fish that get scooped into the net and have not the sense to swim out at once are pushed by the flow of water into the fingerlike tip of the net, the so-called cod end. Few escape from it. When the trawl is hauled to the surface by a winch, all sorts of sea things pour out of the cod end and into the boat. There are usually cod and haddock, often pollock. Among them may be lobsters and scallops from the bottom, flatfish including halibut, and many kinds of trash fish for which there is no market. Some of them are oddities from the lower depths with enormous eyes and jaws and phosphorescent organs that glow bright in the dark. The trash fish are thrown overboard; the valuable fish are cleaned at once and then they are packed in shaved ice in the hold.

When a trawl comes to the surface, sea gulls gather in a screaming cloud to grab the offal and trash fish. Every trawler has its retinue of gulls —except the Russian ones. The great Soviet factory ships use every part of every fish that their trawlers catch. They discharge nothing but dirty water into the sea, so the gulls take no interest in them. Hostile shore-front critics claim the Russians feed heads, guts and all to their hungry people. A more charitable view is that they use the less pleasant parts to make fish meal for Russian chickens.

Fish that swim in schools at the surface, such as mackerel, are caught commercially in purse seines—long, fencelike nets that hang vertically in the water with floats on the upper edge and weights on the lower edge. The fishermen are sometimes guided to a school by the sea birds hovering over it, or by airplane spotting. They circle the school, paying out the net. It never occurs to the fish to dive under it, so they are caught in the "purse" when the lower edge is gathered together and are pulled, sometimes many tons of them, into the boat.

Swordfish, which many connoisseurs consider the king of fish, were formerly harpooned while sleeping on the surface. Some sport fishermen still use this method, but most commercial swordfishing is now done with "long-lines" developed by the Japanese. The lines are stout ropes as much as 10 miles long supported by buoys every 600 feet or so. Short lines with baited hooks are attached at intervals and reach down 100 to 200 feet below the surface where swordfish do most of their feeding. The lines are left dangling there from 4 to 12 hours. When the lines are winched in, gigantic swordfish, their sharp swords slashing savagely, come up on the five-inch hooks. It takes skilled and courageous men with clubs to subdue these monsters on deck.

A replica of a cod—a regional trademark—tops a weather vane above the Chatham fish pier on Cape Cod. Providing a livelihood for generations of fishermen, the cod is all but sacred in parts of New England. The Pilgrims named the cape for it because the fish were so plentiful in the waters nearby.

Many people have no idea how good swordfish can be because they have never eaten anything but the frozen kind. This is what most restaurants must serve, and swordfish does not take kindly to freezing, which makes it dry out in cooking. Even when inlanders buy fresh swordfish they do not know how to select it. Salesmen in fish markets often try to push upon unwary customers the steaks cut from the forward end of the fish, and these include a lot of dark fat and the flesh that surrounds the abdominal cavity. It looks all right but is flabby and lacks proper flavor. In spite of any resistance from the salesman, you should insist on solid muscle cut from the tail astern of the abdomen. This advice also applies to steaks of all other large fish, such as the excellent halibut. Another good rule is to avoid cuts of fresh fish that are wrapped in plastic film. The film keeps you from applying the smell test. The salesman may be irritated with you if you reject his smelly fish, but he will respect you and treat you better next time.

Trawl-caught and seine-caught fish do not have the quality of hooked fish taken ashore the very same day because they are kept on ice for a week or so before they reach port. Even so, they are good if properly iced, shipped promptly to market and not kept too long before they are sold to the consumer. Thousands of tons are flown out of New England and eastern Canada by air freight. Commercial fishery experts claim that the stale, off-flavor fish that are all that so many people know, have sat around for days in groceries and fish markets at temperatures well above the freezing point. Frozen fish is never as good as fresh, but it is far better than this sad, neither-fresh-nor-frozen stuff.

Everyone knows that fish spoil rapidly, but few people stop to wonder why they are so different from beef, which is much like fish in nutritive value but keeps almost indefinitely just above the freezing point. Beef is even improved (ripened) for meat-lovers by being hung for a while at room temperature. But if fish were hung this way, no one would want to smell or eat them.

The reason for the difference is both biological and chemical. Fish at large in the sea are protected from bacteria by a natural layer of slime. When they are caught and die, the slime loses its effectiveness, and bacteria embedded in it attack the skin and flesh. Since they are marine bacteria accustomed to low temperatures, they multiply slowly even while the fish is packed in shaved ice. The bacteria associated with beef and the meat of other warm-blooded animals require comparatively high temperatures to grow, so they can be made inactive by refrigeration.

Even when beef bacteria multiply fast, as they do when beef is hung, they do not produce a spoiled flavor for a rather long time. But fish flesh is slightly different chemically. It contains a small amount of a harmless, odorless and tasteless compound called oxytrimethylamine. Bacteria turn this compound into trimethylamine, which gives off a powerful and disagreeable spoiled fish odor. The flesh is not damaged as food; it is just as wholesome and nutritious as ever, but it has lost its fresh flavor forever. If fresh, unfrozen fish is properly iced and handled, it will keep most of its attractive flavor for about 10 days.

New Englanders and seaboard Canadians are brought up to be fussy

Continued on page 76

On a windy wintry day a fishing trawler, its bow throwing up a plume of spray, chugs out toward Georges Bank.

The New England Fishing Fleet Harvests the Bountiful Waters of Georges Bank

Southeast of Boston, over the horizon from Cape Cod, lies one of the richest fishing grounds of the Atlantic Coast, the great oval-shaped, underwater plateau called Georges Bank. Larger (22,000 square miles) than the state of Massachusetts, it is made up of coarse sand and gravel sediments deposited by the glaciers on the continental shelf. In pre-glacial times it was a forested island. Georges Bank is a dangerous place, with persistent fogs and swift, tricky currents. But in its shallow waters, warmed by the Gulf Stream, ocean fish—cod, haddock, pollock, and the flat fish such as halibut—congregate to spawn and to feed. And so the hardy commercial fishermen from New England's ports are drawn there too, to hunt down food for American tables.

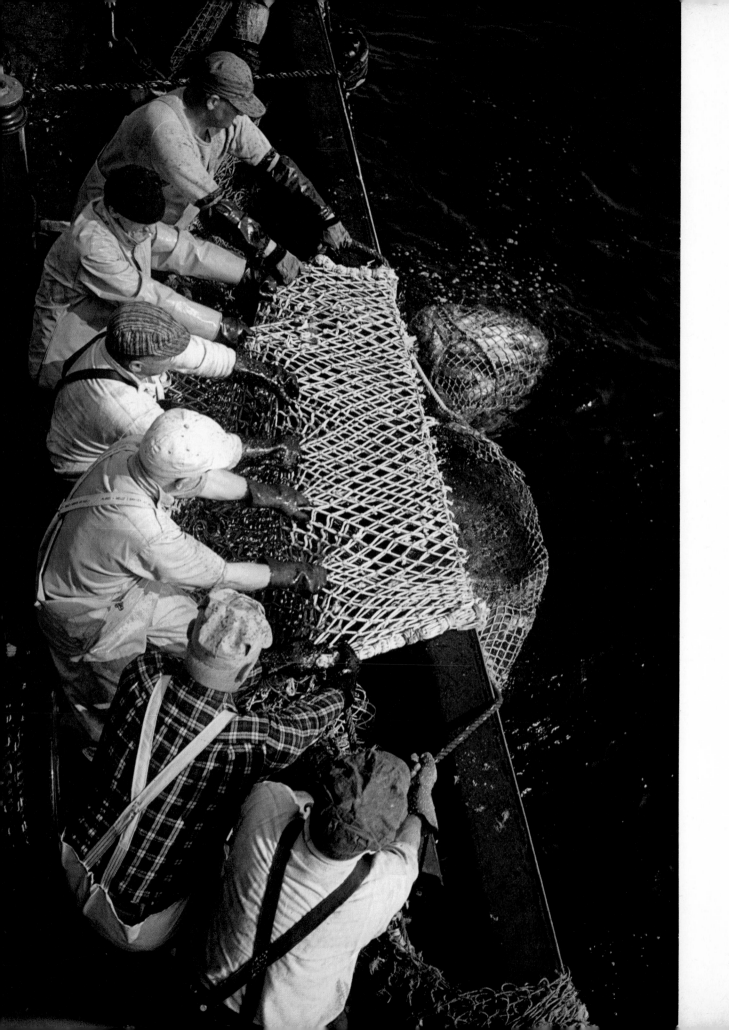

Fishermen eviscerate haddock before putting them on ice for the trip home. (To prevent spoilage, Massachusetts law forbids boats to carry uncleaned fish into port.) The trawlers visit Georges Bank in all seasons, and a fisherman earns up to $14,000 a year, though he may have little time at home.

Aboard a boat at the Georges Bank fishing grounds, fishermen join forces to haul in the otter trawl, a big baglike net with a narrow neck. Such a net can bring up 1,500 pounds of fish at a time. Modern trawlers use sonar and other electronic detecting devices to locate the schools of fish swimming below.

Opposite: At the Boston Fish Pier lumpers unload the dragger *Caracara.* Since her return to port during the night, her entire catch, a mixed one, has been sold on the New England Fish Exchange, housed on the pier. Auctions at the Exchange begin promptly at 7:30 a.m. with the ships' catches posted on big blackboards; ordinarily, bidding is over in less than an hour, and it usually determines New England fish prices across the country. At left, a lumper guides a four-bushel canvas bag of cod out of a hatch onto the pier.

The Favorite Food Fish of New England and Eastern Canada

STRIPED BASS

COD

SCROD (YOUNG COD)

LEMON SOLE

POLLOCK

WHITING

YOUNG POLLOCK

WHITE HAKE

BABY SWORDFISH

BLACKBACK FLOUNDER

ATLANTIC SALMON

SCUP

Shown here are the major food fish caught by commercial fishermen off the northeast coast. Most of the catches are sold and eaten in the New England states and Canada's Atlantic provinces, but some fish are shipped to markets across the country. The fish on these pages look as they would when taken from the water; fish on sale in markets have been eviscerated.

HADDOCK

SCROD (YOUNG HADDOCK)

OCEAN PERCH

HALIBUT

MACKEREL

HERRING

GREY SOLE

YELLOWTAIL FLOUNDER

DAB

about the freshness of their fish, and they usually cook it in ways that do not overwhelm its delicate taste, which is different for each kind of fish. Spices are used sparingly, and strong vegetable flavorings such as garlic and tomato are not part of the native tradition. The exception to this rule is onion, which is usually fried a little to drive off most of its pungency. Although New England has nothing like the French bouillabaisse, some New England cookbooks tell how to make a version of that overflavored dish which is best suited for seafood past its prime. Good fish deserve to be treated with more respect.

Besides frying and broiling, which should be done with small fish and may be done with the fillets and steaks cut from large ones, the best way to cook a really fresh fish is by baking. A four- or five-pound striped bass baked with strips of salt pork or fat bacon draped over it and frequently basted is about the finest offering of the sea. Baked whole cod, haddock and pollock are almost as good. Stuffing is not necessary, but it is a helpful addition that keeps the fish from drying out from the inside.

Baked, boiled or steamed fish calls for a sauce, but since it is not a strongly flavored food, a mild sauce is liked best. This may be drawn butter, traditionally a thin white sauce into which additional butter has been stirred, or an even simpler version with the same name, which is butter alone, heated to the point of foaming. For serving with fish, the former is much improved by mixing with sliced or chopped hard-boiled eggs. The yellow and white pieces of egg and the buttery sauce team up with the fish to produce a magnificent effect. A sprinkling of chives or parsley helps, but do not use too much of it.

Fish chowder is another plain, lightly seasoned way of cooking fish *(Recipe Index)*. It is popular from Connecticut to Newfoundland and probably dates from the time when the first cows in the colonies provided the milk that is its essential ingredient. It varies a good deal from place to place, but the basic recipe starts, as corn chowder does, with diced salt pork. This is rendered, and the fat is then used for frying onions. Next cubed or sliced potatoes are added with a little water and cooked until tender. My mother used to slice them in wedges so the sharp edges would disintegrate and give a little thickening. The fish, usually sizable chunks of cod, haddock or pollock, is then added and simmered only long enough to cook it through. Milk is heated separately and added last.

Most cooks insist on their own variations on this theme. A common one is to use whole fish, including the heads with only the eyes removed. (The eyes do no harm, but even when boiled they have a reproachful look.) When the flesh begins coming apart, it is removed, freed of bones and set aside. The water the fish was cooked in is strained and used to boil the potatoes. Finally the fish and hot milk are added. This variant has more fish flavor, which many people prefer. To make the most elaborate chowder, the onions, potatoes and fish are packed in layers in a kettle and cooked very slowly with a little milk or water. Since the pieces of fish are not stirred or otherwise disturbed, they stay whole. Hot milk is added later, and sometimes strips of browned salt pork are served separately and eaten with the fingers. They are fine, salty accents. Most cooks decry thickening; a few add a little flour and water, but the thick, thick fish chowders that are sometimes served in restaurants are abominations designed to conceal their low fish content.

Proper fish chowder is thin and should be served in a soup plate and eaten with a spoon, but it is too substantial to be considered a soup. Supplemented by a salad and fortified with unsalted common crackers (those round, hard, hollow crackers that cleave in two so easily), it is a whole, large meal. Fish soups are no less excellent, but they are served in smaller quantity (there should always be *lots* of chowder) and the fish in the soups is finely shredded, not preserved in good-sized pieces. Fish stews with tomato, celery, olive oil, garlic and herbs are really Mediterranean, not American. Though recipes for them are found in some Yankee cookbooks, they probably originated with the Portuguese fishermen who are a conspicuous and picturesque feature of many new England ports. Some of these highly flavored dishes are interesting, though the taste of the fish in them is hard to detect.

I suspect that salmon, a noble fish, was never plentiful in southern New England. It early acquired a great-occasion importance, and this is pretty good proof that it was always scarce. The custom was and still is to serve steamed salmon with green peas and new potatoes *(Recipe Index)* on the Fourth of July as a kind of preliminary harvest festival, these vegetables being available at that date. On Cape Cod the custom was rare, presumably because the Cape has no salmon-size rivers, but my mother's Connecticut background led us to serve salmon on the Fourth.

Since I was the tender of the vegetable garden my job was to pick the peas, which were at their best about then, and dig the potatoes. The potato vines were far from mature, and we all felt, New England-like, that none of them should be destroyed at this early stage of their growth. So with a small trowel I carefully loosened the soil around their roots and felt for the young potatoes, none of them bigger than golf balls and many much smaller. It was like feeling around for warm eggs under setting hens. Gently boiled in their tissue-thin skins and garnished with butter and chopped parsley, those delicate infant potatoes were worthy of the noblest salmon. The vines that I had robbed of their young proceeded to form more potatoes.

Whenever I read very old New England cookbooks I get the feeling that Yankees of 200 years ago were forced to eat fish rather too often, and therefore tried to vary the taste by using a great variety of strong-flavored fish sauces. The receipts collected in 1763 by Mrs. Silvester Gardiner of Boston include 23 of them, made of all sorts of ingredients, including anchovies, pickled mushrooms, pickled walnuts, oysters, mussels, lobster, shrimp, lemon peel, vinegar and all the spices then known. Most of them seem pretty strong, and it may well be that the fish of pre-revolutionary Boston were also strong, which would not be surprising considering the slowness of wagon transport and lack of refrigeration. I feel that the fresh and frozen fish made available by modern handling are better without such disguises.

Mrs. Gardiner did not have to rely wholly on dubious fresh fish. She undoubtedly used a great deal of salted or smoked fish, a local product that was so important in her day that a six-foot model of a codfish ("the sacred cod") was hung in the Massachusetts State House, where it has remained for more than 200 years. When properly prepared, dry salt cod will keep almost indefinitely, and thousands of barrels of it were exported by the Yankees to the other American colonies, to Europe, the Caribbean and South America.

Salt codfish (cod is the fish that takes salt best) has its own rather vigorous flavor, and it surely had more when it was dried in the fitful New England sunlight. But its flavor is not in the least like the reek of spoiled fresh fish. Anyone who gets accustomed to it, as generations did, learns to love it and yearn for it.

The ways to cook it are few and simple, none of them as elaborate as *bacalao a la vizcaína,* the famous salt cod dish of northern Spain. The New Englander's first step is to remove most of the salt, which is done either by soaking the fish overnight or by bringing it gently to a boil in two changes of water. The freshened fish is then simmered until it is cooked, which does not take long. In my family it was generally served whole or flaked with cream sauce on toast and decorated with sliced hard-boiled eggs. This is often called Cape Cod turkey and traditionally comes to the table surrounded by boiled potatoes.

A humble but nonetheless excellent salt-fish dish is fish cakes or fish balls. There are various recipes, but the essentials are freshened, simmered and shredded salt codfish mixed with mashed potatoes. Some cooks add an egg, baking powder and a little black pepper. When the mixture is molded into balls and fried in deep fat, it becomes fish balls; pressed into flat cakes and cooked in a frying pan it becomes fish cakes. Both should be golden brown and not greasy and both have a somewhat fuzzy appearance due to the fibers of the fish. They taste wonderful and are fine for breakfast with or without ketchup.

These two good but rather delicate presentations of salt codfish are better suited to sedentary people than to outdoor workers. For the latter a salt-fish dinner, sometimes called a Cape Cod or salt cod boiled dinner *(Recipe Index),* might start with a goodly amount of finely diced salt pork rendered and left floating in its hot grease in a bowl or gravy boat placed at the center of a large platter. Around it was a wide band of freshened and simmered salt cod in a cream sauce. Then came a band of boiled sliced beets (red), a band of turnips (white), one of carrots (orange) and a final band of potatoes (white). A hungry man attacked this colorful masterpiece by heaping his plate high with the things he liked best and pouring the pork scraps and even the grease over them with a ladle. When he finished he knew he had eaten. I enjoyed it most when I was 16, leading a strenuous life and still growing, but even now I like to think about it.

Fried Herring Roe and Milt

Combine the flour, salt and a few grindings of pepper, sift them onto a plate or paper towels and set aside.

In a small skillet, melt 4 tablespoons of the butter over moderate heat, stirring frequently until it turns a nutlike brown. Regulate the heat as necessary to prevent the butter from burning. Set the skillet aside off the heat, covered, to keep the butter warm.

Pat the herring milt sacs and roe completely dry with paper towels. Gently roll the sacs about in the flour mixture to coat them on all sides, and shake off the excess flour.

Immediately melt the remaining 3 tablespoons of butter with the oil in a heavy 10-inch skillet. When the foam begins to subside, add the milt sacs and, turning them with a slotted spatula, fry over high heat for about 2 minutes on each side until they are golden brown. As they brown, transfer them to paper towels to drain.

Gently roll the herring roe about in the flour and shake off the excess, then add the roe to the fat remaining in the pan. Fry the roe for about 1 minute on each side, then drain it briefly on paper towels.

Arrange the fried herring milt and roe attractively on a heated platter or individual serving plates and pour the browned butter evenly over them. Scatter the chopped parsley on top and garnish the platter or plates with the lemon wedges. Serve at once.

To serve 4 as a first course, 2 as a main course

1 cup flour
1 teaspoon salt
Freshly ground black pepper
7 tablespoons butter
½ pound fresh herring milt in its sacs
½ pound fresh herring roe
1 tablespoon vegetable oil
1 tablespoon finely chopped fresh parsley
1 lemon, cut lengthwise into 4 or 8 wedges

Fresh herring milt and roe are a New England spring specialty, to be fried briefly and served promptly with browned butter.

To serve 6

A 6-pound striped bass, cleaned but
  with head and tail left on
1 tablespoon butter, softened plus 6
  tablespoons butter, melted
4 medium-sized firm ripe tomatoes,
  stemmed and cut crosswise into
  ¼-inch-thick slices
2 large onions, peeled and cut
  crosswise into ¼-inch-thick
  slices (about 2 cups)
1 medium-sized green bell pepper,
  cut lengthwise into quarters,
  seeded, deribbed, and sliced into
  ¼-inch-wide strips (about 1
  cup)
½ cup finely chopped fresh parsley
1 teaspoon finely cut fresh tarragon,
  or substitute ½ teaspoon
  crumbled dried tarragon
½ teaspoon finely chopped garlic
2 teaspoons salt
Freshly ground black pepper
¼ cup flour

Tomato-stuffed Striped Bass

Have the fish dealer remove the backbone from the bass, or do it yourself
in the following fashion: Lay the fish flat and fold back the edges of the
cavity opening so that you can easily get at the inside of the fish. With a
sharp boning knife, cut lengthwise along each side of the backbone to separate it from the small rib bones. Leave the rib bones intact and be careful
not to cut the skin. Cut to within about 1 inch of the head and tail and
sever the backbone at these points. Grasping the fish firmly, pull out and
discard the backbone. Wash the bass under cold water and pat it dry inside and out with paper towels. Preheat the oven to 450°. Brush the softened butter over the bottom of a shallow baking dish large enough to
hold the bass comfortably. Combine the tomatoes, onions, green pepper,
parsley, tarragon, garlic, 1 teaspoon of the salt and ¼ teaspoon of black
pepper in a bowl, and toss together. Loosely fill the bass with the stuffing,
then close the opening with small skewers and kitchen cord.

Rub both sides of the fish with the flour and place the fish in the buttered dish. Score the top of the fish by making 3 or 4 diagonal slits about
¼ inch deep, 2 inches long and 1 inch apart. Brush the bass with 2
tablespoons of melted butter and sprinkle it with the remaining salt and
a little black pepper. Bake the fish in the middle of the oven for about 40
minutes, basting it every 10 minutes with the remaining melted butter,
until the fish feels firm to the touch and the skin is brown and crisp.
Serve at once, directly from the baking dish or from a heated platter.

Atlantic salmon poached whole is
the proud dish with which proper
Yankees celebrate the Fourth of
July. Now something of a rarity, the
salmon is found only in coastal
rivers from Cape Sable to Cape Cod
and only in midsummer. Its classic
accompaniments, as time honored as
the salmon itself, are fresh garden
peas, new potatoes and a butter-
cream sauce enriched with bits of
hard-cooked egg. Here it is also
garnished with sprigs of fresh dill.

Cape Cod Boiled Dinner

Starting a day ahead, place the cod in a glass, enameled or stainless-steel bowl, cover it with cold water and soak for at least 12 hours, changing the water 3 or 4 times. Drain the cod and rinse under cold running water. Place the cod in a saucepan and add enough fresh water to cover it by 1 inch. Bring to a boil over high heat. (Taste the water. If it seems very salty, drain, cover the cod with fresh water, and bring to a boil.) Reduce the heat to low and simmer uncovered for 20 minutes, or until the fish flakes easily when prodded with a fork. Drain and cut the fish into 2-by-4-inch pieces. In a heavy 1- to 2-quart saucepan, melt the butter over moderate heat. When the foam begins to subside, stir in the flour and mustard and mix thoroughly. Pour in the milk and, stirring constantly with a whisk, cook over high heat until the sauce comes to a boil and thickens heavily. Reduce the heat and simmer for about 3 minutes to remove the raw taste of flour. Then add the salt and pepper. Taste for seasoning.

In a heavy 8- to 10-inch skillet, fry the salt pork over moderate heat, turning the slices frequently until the pork is crisp and brown on both sides. Transfer it to paper towels to drain and discard the fat in the skillet. Mound the cod on a heated platter and pour the sauce over it. Place the hard-cooked egg slices on top of the fish, arrange the pork slices, potatoes, beets, carrots and rutabaga pieces around it and serve at once.

NOTE: For preparation of the hot vegetables, see the recipe for New England boiled dinner.

2 pounds salt cod
3 tablespoons butter
2 tablespoons flour
1 teaspoon dry mustard
1 cup milk
¼ teaspoon salt
⅛ teaspoon ground white pepper
6 thin 1-by-3-inch slices lean salt pork
3 hard-cooked eggs, cut crosswise into ¼-inch-thick slices
6 medium-sized potatoes, peeled and boiled
6 medium-sized beets, boiled and peeled
12 small carrots, scraped and boiled
1 rutabaga peeled, quartered, cut crosswise into ½-inch-thick slices and boiled

To serve 8 to 10

SALMON

1½ pounds fish trimmings: the
    heads, tails and bones of any firm,
    white-fleshed fish
4 quarts water
2 tablespoons strained fresh lemon
    juice
1 large bay leaf
½ teaspoon whole black
    peppercorns
1 tablespoon salt
A 6- to 7-pound salmon, cleaned,
    with head and tail left on

EGG SAUCE

6 tablespoons butter
½ cup flour
1 quart milk
1 teaspoon salt
¼ teaspoon ground white pepper
8 hard-cooked eggs, coarsely
    chopped
Fresh dill sprigs

Poached Fourth-of-July Salmon

Combine the fish trimmings, water, lemon juice, bay leaf, peppercorns and 1 tablespoon of salt in a 6- to 7-quart enameled or stainless-steel saucepan and bring to a boil over high heat. Reduce the heat to low and simmer partially covered for 20 minutes.

Strain the liquid through a fine sieve into a 12-quart fish poacher or a large, deep roasting pan equipped with a cover. Discard the fish trimmings and the seasonings.

Wash the salmon inside and out under cold running water. Without drying it, wrap it in a long double thickness of dampened cheesecloth, leaving at least 6 inches of cloth at each end to serve as handles for lifting the fish in and out of the poacher or roasting pan.

Twist the ends of the cloth close to the fish and tie them tightly with string, then place the salmon on the rack of the poacher or roasting pan and lower the rack into the poaching liquid. Tie the ends of the cheesecloth to the poacher rack or the handles of the roasting pan. The cooking liquid should cover the salmon by at least 2 inches; add more water to the pan if it is necessary.

Place the lid on the poacher or pan, bring the liquid to a simmer over moderate heat and immediately reduce the heat to low. Simmer gently for 30 to 40 minutes, or until the salmon feels firm when prodded gently with a finger.

Meanwhile, prepare the egg sauce in the following fashion: In a heavy 2- to 3-quart saucepan, melt the butter over moderate heat. When the foam begins to subside, stir in the flour and mix together thoroughly with a wire whisk.

Pour in the milk and, stirring constantly with the whisk, cook over high heat until the sauce comes to a boil and thickens heavily. Reduce the heat to low, whisk in 1 teaspoon of salt and the white pepper, and simmer for 10 to 15 minutes, stirring from time to time. Remove the pan from the heat, taste the sauce for seasoning and gently stir in the hard-cooked eggs. Cover to keep the egg sauce warm.

When the salmon is poached, lift it off the rack, using the cheesecloth ends as handles. Lay the salmon on a large cutting board or platter and open the cheesecloth. With a small, sharp knife, skin the top surface of the fish and scrape off and discard any gray fat clinging to it. Holding both ends of the cheesecloth, carefully lift the salmon and turn it over onto a large heated serving platter. Peel the skin from the upturned side and scrape off the fat.

To serve, garnish the salmon with sprigs of dill and present the egg sauce in a bowl or sauceboat. Or pour half of the egg sauce over the salmon, masking it completely, and serve the remaining sauce separately in a sauceboat.

Traditionally, poached salmon with egg sauce is served on the Fourth of July, accompanied by fresh green peas and boiled new potatoes.

NOTE: For the most predictable results, measure the thickness of the fish before you wrap and poach it. Lay the salmon on its side on a flat surface and insert a metal skewer completely through the fish at its thickest point. Calculate the thickness in inches, and poach the salmon for 10 minutes per inch.

IV

Clambakes and Lobster Feasts

Long before primitive men learned to catch many roundfish, which are agile and elusive, they searched the seashore at low tide for sluggish shellfish that could not swim away. Inside each shell was a squashy creature without much personality but eminently edible. Some were attached to rocks or gravel; others crawled slowly; others lived under the mud or sand. In ancient times they were eaten in such quantity that nearly every long-inhabited shore has great mounds of shells (kitchen middens) that mark where people lived for generations, tossing aside the refuse of their inexhaustible food supply.

New England and eastern Canada still have plenty of these anciently admired foods. It is safe to say that every place at tidewater that can have clams, mussels, scallops or oysters will have them, unless shifting currents or changes in the sea bed keep them away. At the breeding season of each species the water that washes the shore is turbid with the eggs and feebly swimming larvae. Only one in a million escapes being eaten by larger sea creatures and grows big enough to settle down, but so numerous are the young that each suitable settling spot, be it sand, rock or mud, gets its thin-shelled infant claimant striving desperately to stay alive.

When I was a boy on Cape Cod, and much later too, one of my favorite occupations was digging soft or steamer clams on sandflats exposed at low tide. They live well under the sand with their long, extensible necks reaching up just below the surface. In the neck are two channels; through one the clam draws sea water laden with nutritious particles. Through the other it discharges water from which it has filtered the nu-

85

In the dawn's vague light on the first of October, opening day of Cape Cod's six-month scallop season, people of Orleans, Massachusetts dredge for small, succulent bay scallops in the shallow waters of Pleasant Bay. Anyone can buy a license permitting him to gather scallops (usually 1¾ bushels a week); they must be mature ones that show a dark growth ring on their shells.

trients. This way of life is so successful that the clam has survived with little change for perhaps half a billion years, but it has a drawback useful to clam diggers. As I walked the flats I watched for little jets of water squirting out of holes. This giveaway meant that clams below had felt the sandquakes of my approaching footsteps and were drawing down their necks and clenching their shells in anticipation of trouble. There I dug, sometimes with my hands (which resulted in cut fingertips), sometimes with a clam digger, a hoelike implement with flat tines instead of a solid blade. In most of the holes I found a clam. I avoided holes that did not squirt; they might contain horrible creatures such as long, writhing sea worms with dangerous-looking heads and rippling fringe on their sides.

Soft clams are a gift of the gods, but they need informed handling. When freshly dug their round stomachs, which are not exactly stomachs, contain the food they have just filtered out of the water, so the clams should be kept in clear sea water or salted fresh water for a while to give them a chance to get rid of it. Then they should be steamed. Just put them in a covered kettle with a little water and heat rapidly. For added flavor sauté some onions and chopped parsley in butter and add this to the clams and water. There is no danger of their burning because they eject a lot of juice. Take them off the heat when the shells have opened a little way. The juice that comes out is a fine-flavored drink by itself and does wonders for tomato or other vegetable juice.

At a feast of steamed clams each guest should have two plates, one for clams, the other for shells, and a small, deep container such as a custard cup half-full of melted butter. Just open the shell and take the clam out by the neck, which is surrounded by a loose membrane that should be discarded. Some people cut or bite off the black tip of the neck, but this is necessary only if the clam is very large and the tip thus is tough. Dip everything in melted butter and pop it into your mouth. For those who have never tried steamed clams, I guarantee a sensation. Some dedicated clam eaters sit for hours in silence performing this ritual, pausing only to call for more clams and butter and to push heaped-up shells away.

Those who do not dig their own clams should be choosy when buying them. Clams are hardy creatures; they live a long time out of water, but they spoil soon after they die. If you see a clam with its neck extended limply it is dead, and you should reject the whole batch; the others are probably close to death. A clam with loosely clenched shells is suspect. The way to test whether it is alive is to pick it up and touch the tip of the neck, which can be seen at the more pointed end of the shell. If it moves even a little, the clam is alive though probably not "as happy as a clam."

An especially delicious kind of steamed clam is produced by the Indian clambake, an old custom. In summertime New England and parts of eastern Canada are fragrant with clambakes, and they do not have to be near the shore. There are commercial clambakes that anyone may attend, family clambakes, and fraternal clambakes organized by clubs, churches, volunteer fire departments and old-home-week associations. If large, these affairs are generally conducted by semi-professionals who are almost always men. A clambake for 400 people with all the fixings—corn on the cob, chicken, onions, fish, sometimes lobster—is work too heavy for the ladies of the Congregational Church.

For a large midday clambake the preparations start early in the morning when great quantities of firewood and stones are stacked in a neat rectangular pile. The clams must be washed and soaked in fresh water, some of which they absorb; this makes them juicier. Corn must be husked, onions peeled, fish cut in pieces and put in little paper bags. All this is done in an amiable, festival atmosphere. Sometimes the high-school band is playing. The workers joke with their friends and neighbors. The fire is lit and flames grandly. When it burns down, the hot stones are covered with a truckload of wet seaweed. The clams and other foods are piled in wire-bottomed boxes on the steaming weed and covered with tarpaulins. After a while wonderful fragrances steal out with wisps of steam, and everybody gets wolfishly hungry. At last the bake is opened; the guests sit down at long tables, and serious eating begins.

Clambakes do not have to be large. They are successful with only a dozen cantaloupe-sized stones and enough firewood to get them good and hot. A couple of bushels of seaweed is plenty. The best is rockweed, the kind with little rubbery air floats, but other kinds will give much the same salt-water flavor. Clams and other foods can also be baked in a steel barrel, drum or ash can dug partway into the earth or sand to help keep the heat in. Hot stones (best handled with a pitchfork) go in the bottom; then six inches of seaweed; then the clams; then the other foods. The clams should go in first because they provide the moisture for the steam. More seaweed is put on top and the barrel is covered tightly. It takes experience to know when the various foods will be properly cooked, but there is no law against poking to find out. For small families, clams can be steamed in a very large kettle half-full of seaweed and resting on a campfire or even on the kitchen stove. This is cutting corners, but the clams do get a good deal of that seaweed flavor.

Steaming is not the only way to prepare steamer clams. Probably more are eaten in clam chowder, which is made rather like fish chowder but with differences. For a chowder, clams require more preparation than fish. They may be lightly steamed to make the shells open or simply cut open and the soft stomachs set aside. If you are using steamer clams, the black part of the neck is cut off and discarded. It is not really tough, but its blackness mars the beauty of a chowder. The remaining firm parts are chopped coarsely and combined with the soft parts. The other precaution is that if clam broth (the juice from steamed clams) is used to add flavor, the milk for the chowder should be heated separately and added last; the broth tends to make it curdle. I believe clam chowder is the best chowder; it is even good, though not *as* good, made with canned clams.

Besides the soft clam or steamer we have the hard clam or quahog (pronounced co-hog or co-hawg) whose singularly inappropriate zoological name is *Venus mercenaria*. The shells are thick and strong, and inside each is a spot of bright purple. White or purple bits of quahog shell

—chopped, ground and drilled with primitive tools—were the favored material for the beaded wampum that the Indians used for money.

Quahogs prefer mud to sand and usually live below the level of low tide. They can be found by treading (feeling for them with bare feet). Sometimes the treaders work in water to their armpits, bringing up clams with long-handled rakes and placing them in baskets supported by inflated inner tubes. Various other devices can be used when clamming from boats. The most efficient, which requires a pretty big boat, has powerful water jets that blast the clams out of the mud. It can be used for any kind of clam but is prohibited in many places because it puts individual clam diggers out of business.

Quahogs are best when small. The smallest of all are known as littlenecks, after Little Neck, Long Island; they have no necks, and are offered in restaurants on the half shell at large prices. (The Pacific Northwest has its own littleneck, not the same clam.) Slightly larger ones are called cherrystones. Four-inch quahogs are still tender enough to eat steamed, but larger ones are so tough that most of their inner parts must be chopped fine or ground.

Both kinds of clams are cooked in innumerable ways. Fried clams are the most popular in restaurants. They are troublesome to prepare on a small scale, but for a kitchen equipped with a large, thermostatically controlled vat of cooking fat, they are an easy short-order dish. For home cooking, clam fritters, scalloped clams, clam pies and clam cakes are much better. If you try clam cakes made at home, you will be surprised how good they are. They have no resemblance to store-bought frozen clam cakes or sticks. The Lord only knows what those things have in them; the clam meat, if any, is ground so fine it defies identification.

Anyone who strolls the beaches will encounter two other kinds of clam that are not often eaten. Along with the soft clams live razor clams with long, narrow shells like the blades of old-fashioned straight razors. They are hard to dig because they are equipped with a marvelous escape device: a finger of flesh extending from the bottom end of the shell. The clam can make the finger slender and poke it deep into the sand. When danger threatens, the clam reshapes the tip of the finger into a sort of mushroom anchor or grappling iron and pulls itself down. It can repeat the process faster than most diggers can dig, so although "razor fish" are edible, few people get to eat them.

Far out on the surfbeaten sandbars, exposed only at the lowest tides, live the great sea clams whose shells the Indians used as hoe blades. Actually oversized quahogs, they are sometimes called "hens," an old English name for *Venus mercenaria*. I think of them as ash-tray clams; their shells, which grow more than six inches long, are taken home as ash trays by innumerable summer visitors. But if those visitors try to eat sea clams they are disappointed. The soft parts are gritty with sand and most of the hard parts are as tough as chunks carved off a truck tire. I suspect, however, that they are made to serve a culinary purpose in the so-called Manhattan clam chowder, that highly seasoned clam soup made largely of tomatoes, celery, peppers and other cheap vegetables. It is served in the less admirable restaurants of southern New England but is probably of recent Med-

iterranean origin. The few bits of clam it contains have been softened by long boiling, but some of them are still tough. They were probably ground-up old quahogs or tough hens.

It is interesting that mussels play little part in the traditional New England cuisine, though they are enormously plentiful nearly everywhere and can be picked off gravelly creek beds, rocks and wharf piles with almost no effort. Old-style New Englanders considered them poisonous or at least inedible. Many still do.

At an early stage of my married life my wife and I had little money and the weekly food budget often ran out before the end of the week. But we had a valuable bit of knowledge. A friend of mine, a poet, spent a year in a small English coastal town and returned with the report that the local people rejected clams as poisonous—but ate mussels eagerly. He concluded that both clams and mussels are good to eat and acted accordingly. So did we. On many a Saturday or Sunday I went down to Sandwich harbor at low tide and in 15 minutes picked up enough large, blue, perfect mussels to fill a 10-quart pail.

They were delicious lifesavers. We steamed them like soft clams, made chowder of them or broiled them with a little butter on the half shell after light steaming to make them open. We did not know at the time any of the excellent European ways to deal with mussels. The simplest and perhaps the best is to add a little wine and garlic to the pot in which they are steamed. If such flavored mussels are then broiled with butter they are really magnificent.

There are excellent oysters north of the southern boundary of New England, a line which I arbitrarily draw along the middle of Long Island Sound. Cape Cod also has famous ones, and others are found in scattered places as far north as the Gulf of Saint Lawrence, where the plump and delicious Malpeque oyster thrives in the streams that lead into Malpeque Bay on Prince Edward Island. But oysters are not as ubiquitous as clams, and few traditional ways of cooking them have been developed that are not more convincingly claimed by other parts of the United States, or indeed by places in Europe. One dish that I do consider characteristic of New England is scalloped oysters *(Recipe Index)*, which were admired in Boston more than 200 years ago. They are merely shucked oysters baked with a little cream, bread crumbs and butter. They got their name because they were originally baked in large scallop shells. This is nice, but any baking dish or casserole will do just as well and the bread crumbs make the flavor of a modest quantity go a long way. Another good New England way to stretch oysters is Rhode Island oyster pie, which is raw shucked oysters mixed with butter-rich cream sauce, covered with squares of biscuit dough and baked until the dough turns into oystery biscuits.

Since oysters have no fat they benefit from cooking with at least a little fat. I have mightily enjoyed oysters sautéed briefly with butter and a touch of lemon juice. Oysters wrapped in bacon and broiled, or topped with squares of bacon and broiled in their own shells, are luxurious appetizers. I have had these good things in New England and in Canada too, but I do not know, or at least cannot prove, where they originated.

One of my pleasantest youthful memories is of swimming along under-

Opposite: Out of the depths and shallows of New England's coastal waters comes a munificent bounty of crustaceans and mollusks, a selection of which is spread on a bed of seaweed. Going clockwise, from the decorative starfish at top left, the edible seafood includes:

1 Large-clawed North American lobster
2 Sea scallop
3 Maine red shrimp
4 Two soft-shell Ipswich clams, also called steamer clams
5 Cape or bay scallop (shell)
6 Large surf or sea clam, sometimes known as a chowder or "bake" clam
7 Maine red shrimp
8 Oyster
9 Rock crab
10 Two medium-sized hard-shell or cherrystone clams; the largest of these hard-shell clams is usually called simply a quahog; the smallest size is regionally referred to as a littleneck clam
11 Two mussels
12 Spider crab

Overleaf: At the table, seafood cooked and served in its own shells has an extra measure of marine flavor. At left are a trio of stuffed Digby sea scallops, named for a Nova Scotia area and baked with cream, and half a dozen stuffed quahogs. The clam meat is ground, blended with onions, herbs and crumbs, then baked in the shells. At right are two majestic specially cut lobsters done in Locke-Ober's Savannah style: boiled, prepared with a sauce including green peppers, mushrooms and cognac, and then served hot from the oven. All are in the Recipe Index.

water close to the edge of a thicket of eelgrass and watching scallops fly up like quail from a field of corn stover. Scallops are wonderfully active mollusks. They are built like clams with two shells hinged together, but in spite of this plan so admirably adapted to a sedentary life, they flit as blithely as birds. They do it by squirting water jets through holes in their mantles, the membrane between the edges of the shells. The mantle has a fringe of short sensory tentacles and a row of 40 or more tiny blue eyes so the scallop can feel and see where it is going. Normally it moves slowly, edge forward, propelled by gentle jets. Some scallops make shallow nests in the sand by jetting in a tight circle. But when danger approaches, the scallop claps its shells rapidly together and soars away, hinge forward. This escape mechanism is responsible for the scallop's success in life, permitting it to elude whelks, starfish and other enemies of sedentary mollusks. It can even escape codfish by jetting into a tangle of eelgrass.

The scallop's swimming equipment is what makes it so attractive as human food. The water jets get their power from a single large muscle that connects the shells and permits them to be forcibly opened and closed. This muscle is what we call the scallop, and it is the part we eat. The rest of the creature is edible and is eaten in some countries, but in the United States and Canada it is thrown away along with the beautiful shells, whose flutings were designed by nature to give them strength combined with the lightness needed for the scallop's active life.

The little bay scallops whose shells grow to be about three inches across come chiefly from Cape Cod and farther south. They are the most delicious and bring the highest price. Since they are not sedentary, they are not dug like clams or gathered up like oysters. They have to be netted like fish; this is done with small trawllike devices pulled behind boats. Bay scallops live only about two years, and during the season when catching them is permitted, two generations are normally present. The nets are made with interwoven metal rings that hold adult scallops; the little ones slip through the meshes or are sorted out onboard and get a chance to grow bigger for the next scalloping season.

Bay scallops are only the beginning of the scallop family. There are hundreds of species living all over the ocean, and all of them are edible. The most important in the eastern United States are the big sea scallops taken in deep water by large trawls that scrape the bottom. Their shells, which are not fluted, may be eight inches across, and their swimming muscles are sizable hunks of meat. Canada has the Digby scallop, which is intermediate in size between the sea and bay scallops.

Scallops are the ideal raw material for cooks who like to "try things." Inside the shell they are all meat, and only one kind of meat—no waste at all. They are easy to handle; they do not come apart like clams or shrink to nothing like overcooked oysters. And they have a distinctive, vigorous flavor that overrides all competition. A scallop dish cooked with garlic and a battery of herbs is still a scallop dish. But if you want to find out what scallops really taste like, try eating them—the little bay scallops, that is—raw with no condiment except a touch of lemon juice, the way you eat oysters or cherrystone clams. You will be glad that scallops ventured out of the mud a couple of hundred million years ago, learned to swim and developed that powerful swimming muscle for you to enjoy.

The commonest way to serve scallops is thickly breaded and fried in deep fat. This is a favorite with restaurants whose strategists know that cracker crumbs and vegetable oil are cheaper than scallop meat. A better and easier way is to dry them with a towel, roll them lightly in cracker crumbs and broil them briefly with a lot of butter in the pan. The crumbs absorb the juice and some of the butter. For best results the scallops should be spaced out, not jammed together, when broiled.

Scallops can be broiled on skewers with squares of bacon between them, a princely offering at backyard cookouts. They make superlative chowder along the line of clam chowder, and also fine stew made like oyster stew. They can be scalloped like oysters or made into many kinds of combination dishes: with clams, fish, shrimp, oysters or lobster. If large sea scallops are used, they should be cut in two across the grain, which runs from flat side to flat side. Sometimes they have a small bit of tough tissue that should be removed. As long as you remember that overcooking toughens them, it is hard to go wrong with scallops.

The king of shellfish is, of course, the lobster. It deserves the title legitimately—and also it has unfortunately become so expensive that it serves as a symbol of conspicuous consumption for people who value king-size costliness for its own sake.

The big-clawed lobster (those without big claws are known as spiny lobsters or *langoustes*) lives sparsely in northern Europe and along the middle Atlantic seaboard of the United States, but its happiest habitat is colder waters, as far as Labrador. Apparently lobsters can live almost forever. When they reach the weight of five pounds or so, hardly anything attacks them; they just grow bigger and bigger. There are reports from the early days of lobsters six feet long, and monsters weighing 20 to 30 pounds are still pulled up from deep water. They are formidable beasts; their great crusher claws, as big as pork shoulders, can easily crack the bones of a human hand. Such were the lobsters that the early settlers lifted out of the sea with wooden crooks. These specimens had been living just off the shoreline, lords of all they surveyed, until the Europeans arrived. Some were probably centenarians. Once these ponderous veterans had been caught, it would have taken a century of protection to restore the lobster population to its original condition.

Lobsters average much smaller in size now, and in some places they have been almost exterminated by overfishing. But along most of the North Atlantic coast they are still numerous, and the ocean's annual production of lobster meat is probably as great as ever.

Maine is most famous for lobsters, but large quantities also come from Canada's Maritime Provinces. Except for those dredged up by trawlers from deep offshore waters, they are all caught the same way: in the lath-and-netting lobster pots that are a familiar sight along the shore. Lobster pots (called traps in Maine) have changed only a little in more than 100 years. They have two compartments. The inner one, the "bedroom" or "parlor," is baited with the remains of fish from which boneless fillets have been sliced for human consumption. The outer compartment has one or two funnels of nylon netting leading into it. Lobsters attracted by

Continued on page 98

The Ancient Ritual of an Indian Clambake

When the Pilgrims landed in Massachusetts, they found the Indians cooking the local long-neck clams by a time-honored method: steaming them over hot stones covered with seaweed. The newcomers quickly took up the custom, and today New England towns keep the tradition. Here, at Carver, Massachusetts, men prepare a modern clambake for the annual Old Home Day celebration. Along with clams they have arranged onions, husked corn and cut-up fish in wire-bottom boxes, which they set on the hot stones to be covered with seaweed and then with tarpaulins. When the food has cooked, the men will wade into the mess of husks and seaweed, pull back the tarps and serve the feast.

How to eat a steamer: First gently pull the open clam shells apart.

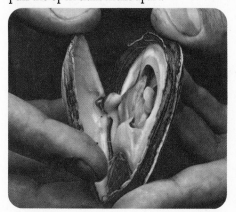

Pull clam out by neck, discarding the tough membrane around neck.

Dunk in broth, then in butter. Discard any that are not open.

the bait skirmish around until they find one of the funnels. They crawl through it eagerly but do not reach the bait until they have passed through another funnel that leads to the bedroom. Not many get out again. Lobsters are not bright enough to look around for the exit. They merely crawl aimlessly, seldom finding the narrow end of the funnel, which is well above the floor of the fatal bedroom.

Lobstering calls for hardy men and is an exciting sport as well as a profession. The coastal waters of Maine with its many bays and islands are dotted, especially in summer, with the bright-painted buoys that mark lobster pots. Every morning chunky little boats go out to tend them, usually with only one man aboard. It is fascinating to watch a skilled Maine lobsterman at work, especially when he is pulling pots set close to a steep shore with the waves foaming over the reefs. He stands amidships within reach of his steering wheel and the engine controls. As he hauls in the pot line, he watches the rocks out of the corner of his eye and moves the wheel a bit, changes engine speed or reverses the propeller to keep the boat from the reef. He lifts a pot over the gunwale, still batting at the controls, opens the hinged top of the pot and takes out the lobsters, if any.

The "shorts" (those whose carapaces, or top shells, are less than the legal minimum of 3¾₁₆ inches long) he tosses back into the water. He also tosses back, with great regret, those with carapaces more than 5 inches long, which may be worth $10 or more but which the state of Maine be-

Off the stony fir-lined shore near Five Islands, Maine, lobster fisherman Maynard Thibodeau pulls one of his baited lobster traps aboard his boat. Thibodeau owns 300 such traps, and hauls up each one of them every other day.

lieves to be valuable as breeders. The in-between others he "plugs," pushing wooden or plastic wedges into the joints of their claws to hold them shut. This should be done at once, for a freshly caught lobster is an angry beast, scuttling around in the boat, its claws held high. With a single snap it can sever the claw of another lobster. If it connects with a human finger, it should never be pulled loose or the sharp teeth will tear the flesh. Just hold it up; the claw will soon relax. Or dip the lobster's tail in water. It will let go, apparently thinking it can now escape.

Successful lobstermen know all about the habits of their prey, and they set their traps in the right places among the rocks where lobsters will pass with the ebb and flow of the tides. Lobsters are bottom feeders; they eat anything living or dead that they can manage, including mollusks, worms, fish, sea urchins, crabs and other lobsters. The big claw is for crushing shells; the small, sharp-toothed claw, which is lighter and more maneuverable, is for catching fast-moving things like fish.

A lobster is clumsy on dry land, but on the sea bottom it is as agile as a rat. Most of its weight is canceled by the support of the water, so it walks lightly on the tips of its eight slender legs. When hunting food it moves cautiously forward, its movable, many-faceted eyes on stalks looking in all directions, and its long antennae probing ahead. Its tail is held straight out behind. When its eyes, antennae or sensory hairs warn the lobster of danger, its tail flaps rapidly and shoots the entire body backward to safety. This vital device is the reason lobster tails are so good to eat. Most of the lobster's meat is in the big muscle that powers that flapping tail.

Lobsters are related to insects, and like insects they wear their rigid skeletons on the outside. This means that they cannot grow without shedding their shells. So in summer the lobsters begin to come apart. First a crack appears at the base of the tail; then the carapace splits. Slowly and arduously the lobster forces itself out through the fissure. The big claw muscles waste away so they can be pulled through the narrow wrist joints. The slender legs, the eyes, the antennae, even the tiny sensory hairs that cover many parts of the shell lose their outer coverings.

The newly moulted lobster is considerably bigger than its old shell —but almost completely helpless. Its soft skin can be broken with a fingernail, and it feels as floppy as jelly. As soon as it gains a little strength, it tries to hide lest eager fish tear it to bits. In this condition, and only in this condition, do the lobsters mate. Lobster emotions are hard to probe so no one knows for sure whether the soft-skinned females are really willing, or whether the males take advantage of their helplessness. One thing is known: large males do not eat small, helpless females with which they mate, though they eat other small lobsters whenever they can catch them.

Female lobsters produce many thousand dark green eggs that look like birdshot and adhere to the swimmerets—the swimming feet—under their tails. In this situation the female is said to be "berried." Maine regulations require that if she is caught she must be returned to the sea so her eggs will get their chance to hatch. When the infants emerge, they are tiny larvae that swim at the surface, moult a few times and gradually get to look more like grown-up lobsters. Then they disappear for a while; they probably seek deep crevices under rocks. They need about seven

Lobsterman Thibodeau holds up two specimens of *Homarus americanus,* the North American or Atlantic lobster, which has two large clawlike pincers.

years to reach the smallest legal size, which for economy's sake is what restaurants prefer to offer.

Lobsters are so expensive nowadays that they are usually served with their shells on so as to make a boiled "chicken" lobster weighing little more than one pound look like a meal for a healthy man, although it contains less meat than a single pork chop. Despite the mild deception, plain boiling is an excellent way to cook them *(Recipe Index)*. Just have a big kettle of boiling salted water and dump the lobsters in. Do not worry about their "agonies"; they do not feel pain in the way that higher animals do, and in any case they are cruel beasts that eat their fellows alive, slowly removing legs, claws, eyes and antennae. Some people in Maine insist that lobsters should be steamed, which is done by putting them in a kettle with half an inch of water in the bottom. I do not recommend this method, especially for softhearted women. The lobsters stir around as the steam hits them, and only gradually quiet down.

It takes a bit of dexterity to eat a boiled lobster with grace and decorum, especially if it is fairly large. The approved way is to break off the tail and the large claws with their arms. Turn the tail on its back and cut its comparatively soft underside longitudinally with a sharp knife. Then the long tail muscle can be removed. It is all edible except for the dark vein on the upper side; this is the alimentary canal, containing whatever the lobster ate last, and it should be removed.

Overlooking the cove at Five Islands, Stephen and Patty Thibodeau and their children, all kin of Maynard *(preceding pages)* enjoy a picnic of boiled lobster dipped in melted butter. At left is 83-year-old Grandfather John Thibodeau, who demonstrates in the pictures on the opposite page his own method of getting out every last delicious morsel of lobster meat.

The claws are a bit more trouble. They should be cracked with a nut-cracker or some sort of hammer (a stone will serve in a pinch). Still better are the strong, short-bladed shears made for the purpose. Both the main part of the claw and its movable part have meat in them, and so do the joints of the arms. These are best reached with shears. The rest of the lobster yields diminishing returns. The carapace contains a small amount of meat, but is hardly worth bothering with unless the lobster is large. The slender legs can be sucked like straws but yield little. Some connoisseurs consider the red "coral" (the immature eggs) and the green liver, also called the tomalley, the best parts of the lobster, but my advice to beginners is to reject the whole carapace. The clear white meat of the tail and claws is best dipped in melted butter. I like to add a little extra salt, and some lobster lovers add a touch of vinegar or lemon juice.

It is a prudent policy to serve attractive backup foods along with lobsters, to divert some attention from their lack of size. Otherwise the marvelous meat is gone only too soon. Another good way to eke out lobsters is to stuff them. In restaurant kitchens they are split alive, the bodies emptied and then refilled with a stuffing of bread crumbs, seasoning and the lobster's chopped coral and liver. Those who do not like the idea of splitting live lobsters can boil them first, and the liver and coral need not be used. The stuffed lobster, with the claws cracked and cut for easy opening, can be either baked *(Recipe Index)* or broiled.

Using your hands, first twist off the lobster's large pincers or claws.

Use a nutcracker to crack the hard shell of the claws in several places.

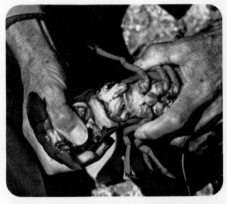
Break off the meaty tail section from the forepart of the lobster's body.

Pull off small tail pieces; suck out meat, which is especially sweet

Inserting thumb or another instrument, push out tail meat.

Pull legs and inner section out of shell and pick out meat inside.

Real clam chowder, New Englanders insist, is made from quahogs and includes milk or cream—never tomatoes.

There are endless ways to cook lobster meat if you do not feel compelled to serve the decorative but inedible shell. Only a few generations ago lobsters were cheap and plentiful enough to be considered a rough, ordinary food, to be eaten in a spirit of fun like hot dogs at a cookout. The Unitarian Church in my home town used to have lobster suppers (my father told me about them, but I think they were even before his time). One or two days before the supper was scheduled, a few church members drove a farm wagon over to Manumet Point about 10 miles away where great weed-covered boulders march out into the sea. They timed their visit for low tide and in a few hours picked up enough lobsters to feed the congregation. The lobsters were not served in their shells. The meat was taken out in a seemly manner behind the scenes and served in one of the many pleasant ways that are possible when it is plentiful.

One way was lobster stew *(Recipe Index),* once a popular dish for political rallies, outings in cool weather and similar large festivities. The stew contained nothing but lobster meat, milk or cream, and butter. To feed hungry countrymen it had to contain a lot of lobsters, but this was no problem when they cost a few cents a pound. It is still wonderfully good but is best treated as an introductory soup. If it is to serve as a main course, lobster stew can be made into a substantial chowder by adding potatoes and onions. In both cases it should be allowed to cool (uncovered, or it may curdle) and ripen for at least 6 hours before reheating for the table. Some cooks enhance the flavor by adding strained water in which the lobster shells have been boiled.

According to the glorious but fast-fading traditions of the state of Maine, lobsters can be fried, made into hash and baked like clams over hot stones and seaweed. All these uses presuppose a brutal amount of lobster meat and hark back to the days when it cost next to nothing. More practical for most people under present conditions are such excellent dishes as scalloped lobster salad. All of them are best if seasonings are held to a whisper so the taste of the lobster can prevail. When this is done, it is hard to go wrong with lobster.

In the past, however, lobster could even be a social error. When my mother's parents bought a house on Cape Cod just before the turn of the century, they made friends with an elderly couple who lived next door and after a proper interval asked them to dinner. My grandparents had been living in New York City where lobsters were already high fashion, and that was what they served as the main dish. But the guests were native Cape Codders operating on a different schedule of time and taste. Lobsters to them were still rough fare. "We don't eat lobster," they announced in unison. When my grandmother recovered from her initial shock, she strained the resources of the kitchen and produced substitute food. This disaster is almost impossible now. Even those few guests who do not like lobster will pretend to like it because of its aura of luxury.

To serve 4

1 medium-sized onion, peeled
¼ cup strained fresh lemon juice
½ teaspoon salt
Freshly ground black pepper
1½ pounds sea scallops,
    thoroughly defrosted if frozen,
    and cut into halves lengthwise if
    they are larger than
    1½ inches in diameter
4 tablespoons butter, melted
1 firm ripe tomato, cut into 8
    wedges
1 lemon, cut into 4 or 8 wedges

Skewered Sea Scallops

Using the second smallest holes of a four-sided grater, grate the onion into a deep bowl. Stir in the lemon juice, salt and a few grindings of pepper. Add the scallops and turn them about with a spoon until evenly coated. Cover the bowl with foil or plastic wrap and marinate the scallops at room temperature for at least 1 hour, or in the refrigerator for 2 hours, turning the scallops over from time to time.

Light a layer of briquettes in a charcoal broiler and let them burn until a white ash appears on the surface, or preheat the broiler of your stove to its highest setting.

Remove the scallops from the marinade and, dividing the pieces evenly, thread them onto 4 long skewers and push the scallops compactly together so that there are no spaces between them. With a pastry brush, thoroughly coat the scallops with the melted butter. Broil about 4 inches from the heat for 8 to 10 minutes, turning the skewers from time to time and basting the scallops frequently with the remaining melted butter. The scallops are done when they are opaque, firm to the touch and flecked all over with brown.

With the side of a knife, slide the scallops off the skewers onto a heated platter or individual plates. Arrange the tomato and lemon wedges attractively around the scallops and serve at once.

To serve 6

1 tablespoon butter, softened,
    plus 4 tablespoons butter,
    plus 2 tablespoons butter, cut
    into ¼-inch bits
½ cup finely chopped onions
1 cup soft fresh crumbs made from
    homemade-type white bread,
    pulverized in a blender or finely
    shredded with a fork
¼ cup finely chopped parsley
2 teaspoons salt
Freshly ground black pepper
6 medium-sized firm ripe tomatoes

Baked Tomatoes

Preheat the oven to 400°. With a pastry brush, spread the tablespoon of softened butter evenly over the bottom and sides of a 13-by-9-by-2½-inch baking dish. Set aside.

In a heavy 8- to 10-inch skillet, melt 2 tablespoons of butter over moderate heat. When the foam begins to subside, add the onions and, stirring frequently, cook for about 5 minutes until they are soft and translucent but not brown. Watch carefully for any sign of burning and regulate the heat accordingly. With a slotted spoon, transfer the sautéed onions to a small mixing bowl.

Melt 2 more tablespoons of butter in the skillet, add the bread crumbs and fry them, stirring frequently until they are golden. Scrape the entire contents of the skillet into the bowl with the onions. Add the parsley, ½ teaspoon of salt and a few grindings of pepper and toss together gently but thoroughly.

Slice the tomatoes in half crosswise. Arrange them cut side up in one layer in the buttered dish. Season with the remaining salt and a few grindings of pepper. Spoon the onion-and-crumb mixture evenly over the tomatoes, and dot the top with the butter bits. Bake in the middle of the oven for about 30 minutes, or until the tomatoes are tender but not limp and the bread crumbs are golden brown.

Serve the tomatoes hot or at room temperature, directly from the baking dish. Or, with a wide metal spatula, arrange the tomatoes attractively on a heated platter.

Clam Chowder

To serve 4

With a sharp knife, chop the tough meat surrounding the soft centers, or stomachs, of the clams and set aside. Cut the soft centers in half and reserve separately on a plate. Strain the clam liquor through a fine sieve lined with a double thickness of dampened cheesecloth and set over a bowl. Measure and set aside 1 cup of the liquor.

Drop the potato dice into enough boiling water to cover them completely and cook briskly until they are tender but still somewhat resistant to the bite. Drain the potatoes in a sieve set over a bowl or pan, and reserve ½ cup of the cooking liquid.

Meanwhile, drop the bacon dice into enough boiling water to cover them completely and boil for 2 minutes. Drain the dice and pat them completely dry with paper towels.

In a heavy 2- to 3-quart saucepan, fry the bacon and 1 tablespoon of butter over moderate heat, stirring frequently until the dice are crisp and brown and have rendered all their fat. With a slotted spoon transfer the dice to paper towels to drain.

Add the onions to the fat remaining in the pan and, stirring frequently, cook for about 5 minutes over moderate heat until they are soft and translucent but not brown. Watch carefully for any sign of burning and regulate the heat accordingly.

Stir in the reserved cup of clam liquor, the ½ cup of potato cooking liquid and the finely chopped clams. Reduce the heat to low, cover tightly and simmer for 10 minutes. Stir in the halved clam centers and continue to simmer covered for 3 minutes longer.

Meanwhile, in a separate saucepan, warm the milk and cream over moderate heat until small bubbles appear around the edge of the pan.

Pour the hot milk and cream into the simmering clam mixture and mix well. Then stir in the thyme, salt, a few grindings of pepper and the drained bacon dice. Taste the chowder and add more salt if needed.

Ladle the chowder into 4 heated soup plates, place a teaspoon of butter on top of each serving, and serve at once.

NOTE: Some New England traditionalists insist that the clam chowder improves in flavor if, after cooking, it is allowed to rest off the heat but unrefrigerated for about an hour and then reheated very briefly just before it is served.

3 dozen hard-shell or littleneck clams (*see page 90*), each about 3 inches in diameter, shucked (about 3 cups), with their liquor or juices reserved
2 medium-sized boiling potatoes, peeled, sliced ½ inch thick and cut into ½-inch dice (about 2 cups)
2 ounces lean slab bacon with rind removed, sliced ¼ inch thick and cut into ¼-inch dice
1 tablespoon plus 4 teaspoons butter
1 cup finely chopped onions
2 cups milk
½ cup light cream
½ teaspoon crumbled dried thyme
½ teaspoon salt
Freshly ground black pepper

The Atlantic sea scallop is found in waters many fathoms deep, and generally is opened, packed and iced on the spot. As shown at far left, it has two saucer-shaped shells hinged at the back; they can be pried open readily. An opened scallop is shown at center; ordinarily only the adductor muscle or "eye" (*right*) is packed for sale. In a large seven- or eight-inch shell, this muscle may be as much as two inches in diameter.

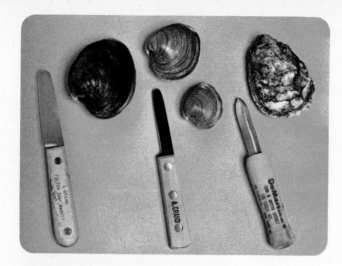

How to Shuck Oysters and Quahogs

Live hard-shell clams and oysters are shut so tightly that you need special knives—and practice—to pry them open. At far left is a sturdy clam knife designed for shucking the large quahog, or chowder clam, efficiently. The more slender-bladed knife at center is for opening the smaller quahogs, the cherrystone *(top)* and littleneck *(bottom)*, which are most often served on the half-shell. The oyster knife shown at near left has a sharp curved tip and a distinctive round handle.

THE SHARP CURVED TIP OF AN OYSTER KNIFE PRIES THE SHELLS OPEN

Seen from the side *(left)*, half of an oyster shell is nearly flat, the other half rounded. To shuck an oyster: (1) grip the narrow end between thumb and fingers, rounded half against your palm. Hold the knife near its point, curved tip down, and insert it near the narrow end. (2) Pressing the knife firmly against the top shell half, cut through to the muscle attached to the center of the shell and then around the rim, holding the shell slightly open with your thumb. (3) Turn the blade, curved tip up, and free the meat and membrane or veil from the top shell half (4) Open the shell and cut the meat from the other shell half. (5) The oyster is now freed and ready to eat.

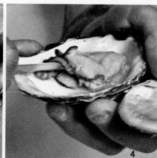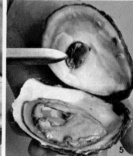

THE FLAT BLADE OF A CLAM KNIFE FORCES THE SHELLS APART

Seen from the side *(left)*, the two shell halves of a quahog are nearly identical. To shuck a quahog: (1) hold the shell lengthwise along your palm with the hinged side away from the knife. Insert the knife blade into the shell near the hinge. (2) Keeping the knife blade firmly pressed against the top half, cut toward the hinge to sever the muscle there. Next cut around the rim, with the knife blade penetrating about ½ inch inside, holding the shell slightly open with your thumb. (3) Now open the clam and free the meat completely from the membrane on the top half. (4) Free the meat from the other shell half. (5) The clam is now ready to be eaten or cooked.

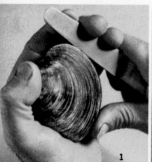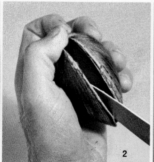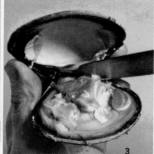

Clam Pie

Preheat the oven to 400°. With a sharp knife, cut the soft centers out of the clams and set them aside on a plate. Chop the remaining tougher clam meat coarsely and reserve it with the clam centers. Strain the clam liquor through a fine sieve lined with a double thickness of dampened cheesecloth. Measure and set aside 1 cup of the liquor.

With a pastry brush, spread the softened butter evenly over the bottom and sides of a 1½- to 2-quart enameled cast-iron casserole. Add the mushrooms, 2 tablespoons of the lemon juice and the salt. Cover tightly and cook over moderate heat for about 10 minutes, or until the mushrooms have given off most of their liquid. Uncover and set aside.

In a heavy 1½- to 2-quart saucepan, melt the 3 tablespoons of butter pieces over moderate heat. When the foam begins to subside, stir in the flour to make a paste. Continue to stir with a wire whisk while you slowly pour in the cup of clam liquor, the white wine, cream and milk. Cook over high heat, still stirring, until the sauce comes to a boil, thickens heavily and is smooth. Reduce the heat to low and simmer for about 3 minutes, then mix in the sherry, the remaining tablespoon of lemon juice and the white pepper. With a slotted spoon remove the reserved clams and mushrooms from their liquid and stir them into the sauce. Taste for seasoning. Then pour the entire mixture into a shallow, round baking dish about 9½ inches in diameter and 2 inches deep.

Following the directions for a pie-crust top *(see short-crust pastry, Recipe Booklet)*, roll the dough into a circle 12 inches in diameter and ⅛ inch thick. Drape the dough over the rolling pin, lift it up, and unroll it over the baking dish. With scissors or a small knife, trim off the excess dough leaving a 1-inch overhang all around the rim. Turn the overhang underneath the edge of the circle and secure the dough to the rim by crimping it tightly with your fingers or a fork.

Cut a 1-inch round hole in the center of the pie and brush the entire pastry surface with the egg-and-milk mixture. Bake in the middle of the oven for 15 minutes, then reduce the oven temperature to 325° and bake for 1 hour longer, or until the crust is golden brown.

Serve at once, directly from the baking dish.

Baked Digby Scallops

Preheat the oven to 350°. With a pastry brush, spread the tablespoon of softened butter over the inside surfaces of 6 large scallop shells or the bottom and sides of a 10-by-6-by-2-inch baking dish. (Arrange the shells, if you are using them, side by side in a jelly-roll pan.) Place the scallops in a bowl, sprinkle them with the salt and a liberal grinding of pepper, and toss with a spoon to season the scallops evenly.

In a heavy 8- to 10-inch skillet, melt the 6 tablespoons of butter over moderate heat. When the foam begins to subside, add the cracker and bread crumbs and stir for 4 or 5 minutes until the crumbs are crisp.

Spread about half the crumbs in the scallop shells or baking dish and scatter the scallops on top. Sprinkle the scallops with the remaining crumbs and pour in the cream. Bake in the middle of the oven for 30 minutes, or until the cream bubbles and the crumbs are golden. Serve at once.

To serve 6

6 dozen small hard-shell or little-neck clams *(see page 90)*, each about 2 inches in diameter, shucked and drained, with their liquor reserved
3 tablespoons butter, softened, plus 3 tablespoons butter cut into small pieces
1 pound fresh mushrooms, trimmed, wiped with a damp cloth, and cut lengthwise into quarters, including the stems
3 tablespoons strained fresh lemon juice
¼ teaspoon salt
¼ cup flour
¼ cup dry white wine
½ cup heavy cream
½ cup milk
2 tablespoons dry sherry
⅛ teaspoon ground white pepper
Short-crust pastry dough for a pie top *(Recipe Booklet)*
1 egg beaten with 1 tablespoon milk

To serve 6

1 tablespoon butter, softened, plus 6 tablespoons butter
1 pound (1 pint) Digby scallops, or substitute large, whole bay scallops or sea scallops, cut into ¾-inch pieces
1 teaspoon salt
Freshly ground black pepper
1½ cups fine crumbs made from unsalted soda crackers, pulverized in a blender or placed between sheets of wax paper and crushed with a rolling pin
½ cup soft fresh crumbs made from homemade-type white bread, pulverized in a blender or finely shredded with a fork
½ cup heavy cream

To serve 4

Four 1½-pound live lobsters
3 tablespoons butter
½ cup thinly sliced fresh
    mushroom caps
¼ cup finely chopped green pepper
2 tablespoons flour
1 cup milk
¼ cup cognac, or substitute ¼ cup
    dry sherry
1 teaspoon paprika
1 teaspoon salt
Freshly ground black pepper
2 tablespoons canned pimiento,
    drained and finely chopped
¼ cup soft fresh crumbs made
    from homemade-type white
    bread, pulverized in a blender or
    finely shredded with a fork
3 tablespoons freshly grated
    imported Parmesan cheese

Locke-Ober's Lobster Savannah

(A specialty of the famous Boston restaurant, which opened in 1875.)
In an 8-quart fish poacher or stock pot, bring 5 quarts of water to a boil
over high heat. Meanwhile, with short lengths of kitchen string, tie the
head, midsection and tail of each lobster to a long wooden spoon as shown
in the photograph opposite. The spoons will hold the shells flat and prevent the tails from curling when the lobsters are boiled.

Plunge 2 lobsters into the pot and return the water to a boil. (The
water should cover the lobsters by at least 1 inch; if necessary, add more
boiling water.) Set the lid on the pot and cook briskly for 15 to 18 minutes. To test for doneness, remove one of the lobsters from the pot and
grasp the end of one of the small legs at either side of the body. Jerk the
lobster sharply. If the body drops away from the leg, the lobster is done.
If the body remains attached to the leg, boil the lobster for 2 or 3 minutes
longer. With tongs, transfer the cooked lobsters to a platter to drain, and
boil the remaining 2 lobsters similarly in the same water.

Cut off all the strings and transfer the lobsters to a cutting board. Then
cut or twist off the antennae and discard them. Twist off the claws of
each lobster at the point where they meet the body, crack each claw in
two or three places with a cleaver, and pick out all the meat. Cut the
lobster meat into ½-inch pieces and reserve it; discard the claw shells.

One at a time place the lobsters on the board. With a sharp boning
knife or heavy kitchen scissors, carefully cut a long oval-shaped opening
out of the back of the shell. Start cutting at the base of the head and fin-
ish cutting just before the fan-shaped tail; depending on the size of the
lobster, make the oval 1½ to 2 inches wide. Reaching through the opening, pick out all the meat from the body and tail. Remove and discard the

COPING WITH A LIVE LOBSTER
Place the lobster on its back and
hold the pegged claws over its head.
With a heavy, sharp knife, cut down
firmly along the middle of the
lobster from a point between the
antennae to the fan-shaped tail,
slicing clean through the back shell.
Open the lobster flat *(right)* and
scoop out and discard the stomach
sac and intestinal vein. Save the
black roe, or coral if there is any as
well as the liver, or tomalley.

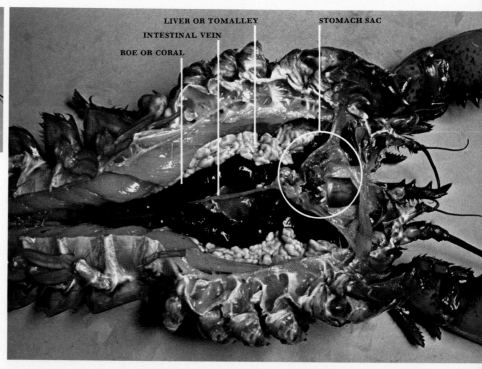

LIVER OR TOMALLEY
INTESTINAL VEIN
ROE OR CORAL
STOMACH SAC

gelatinous sac (stomach) in the head and the long white intestinal vein attached to it. Scoop out the greenish tomalley (liver) and reserve it. Discard the red coral (roe), if there is any. Cut the meat into ½-inch pieces and set the meat and shell aside. (At this point the lobster meat and body shells may be covered tightly with foil or plastic wrap and safely kept in the refrigerator for up to a day.)

Half an hour before you plan to serve the lobsters, preheat the oven to 400°. In a heavy 10- to 12-inch skillet, melt the butter over moderate heat. When the foam begins to subside, add the mushroom caps and green pepper and, stirring frequently, cook for 8 to 10 minutes until the liquid that has accumulated in the pan has almost completely evaporated. Do not let the mushrooms or peppers brown; watch carefully and regulate the heat as necessary.

Stir in the flour and mix well. Then pour in the milk and, stirring constantly with a whisk, cook over high heat until the sauce comes to a boil, thickens lightly and is smooth. Reduce the heat to low and stir in the reserved tomalley, the cognac (or sherry), paprika, salt and a few grindings of pepper. Simmer for about 5 minutes, then add the lobster meat and pimiento and turn them about with a spoon until they are coated with sauce. Taste for seasoning.

Spoon the lobster mixture into the shells, dividing it evenly among them and mounding it attractively. Mix the bread crumbs and grated Parmesan together in a bowl and sprinkle them over the filling. Arrange the shells side by side on a jelly-roll pan and bake in the middle of the oven for 15 minutes, or until the sauce is bubbling and the tops lightly browned. If you like, slide the lobsters under a preheated broiler for 30 seconds or so to brown the tops further. Serve at once.

PREPARING LOBSTER SAVANNAH

Locke-Ober's lobster Savannah (*recipe above*) must be prepared in a special way. Tie the live lobster firmly to a long wooden spoon with lengths of kitchen string (*left*), to keep the shell flat and the tail from curling up. After cooking, cut a long oval-shaped opening in the back of the shell (*center and far right*), using a sharp boning knife or kitchen scissors. Cut an oval about 1½ to 2 inches wide from the base of the head to within ½ inch of the fan-shaped tail. Carefully pick out all the meat from the body and tail with a seafood fork, then remove and discard the stomach sac and intestinal vein, but save the tomalley and any roe. After boiling you may cut or twist off the claws and antennae.

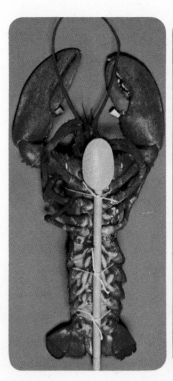  

Nantucket Scallop Chowder

To serve 4

In a heavy 2- to 3-quart saucepan, melt 3 tablespoons of butter over moderate heat. When the foam begins to subside, add the onions and, stirring frequently, cook for about 5 minutes, or until they are soft and translucent but not brown.

Pour in the milk (or milk and light cream) and bring the mixture to a simmer over moderate heat. Reduce the heat to low and simmer partially covered for 15 minutes.

Meanwhile, drop the potato dice into enough lightly salted boiling water to cover them by at least 1 inch and cook briskly until tender. Drain thoroughly and set aside in a bowl.

Melt 2 tablespoons of butter in a heavy 10- to 12-inch skillet. Drop in the scallops and, turning them about almost constantly with a slotted spoon, fry over high heat for 2 or 3 minutes until they are opaque on all sides. Set the scallops aside with the potato dice.

Strain the onion-and-milk mixture through a fine sieve into a bowl; discard the onions and return the liquid to the saucepan. Add the scallops and potato dice and simmer for 2 or 3 minutes to heat them through.

Taste for seasoning and ladle the chowder into heated individual soup bowls. Place one of the remaining 4 teaspoons of butter in each bowl, sprinkle the chowder with a little paprika and serve at once.

5 tablespoons plus 4 teaspoons butter
2 medium-sized onions, peeled and cut crosswise into ¼-inch-thick slices
1 quart milk, or substitute 2 cups milk and 2 cups light cream
1 medium-sized boiling potato, peeled and cut into ½-inch dice (about 1 cup)
Salt
1 pound sea scallops, thoroughly defrosted if frozen, cut against the grain into ¼-inch-thick slices
Paprika

Fried Scallops, Portuguese Style

To serve 2

Wash the scallops quickly under cold running water, then spread them in one layer on a jelly-roll pan covered with a linen towel. Drape a second towel over the scallops and place them in the refrigerator for about 4 hours to drain thoroughly.

In a small, heavy saucepan or skillet, melt the butter over low heat, turning the bits about with a wooden spoon to melt them slowly and completely without letting the butter brown. Remove the pan from the heat and let the butter rest for a minute or so. Then skim off the foam from the surface and discard it.

Tipping the pan at a slight angle, spoon the clear butter on top into a heavy 12-inch skillet (preferably a slope-sided one with a non-stick cooking surface). Leave behind all of the milky solids that will have settled at the bottom of the pan.

Place the flour in a large bowl and drop the scallops into it. With a slotted spoon or your fingers toss the scallops about gently until they are coated on all sides with the flour. Then turn them out into a sieve and shake them vigorously to remove the excess flour.

Warm the clear butter in the skillet over high heat for 10 seconds. Add the scallops and, sliding the pan back and forth to turn them about, fry them for 2 or 3 minutes until they are firm but not brown. Do not overcook the scallops.

Add the chopped garlic and parsley to the skillet and slide the pan vigorously back and forth for about 30 seconds longer.

Mound the scallops attractively on a heated platter, season with the salt and a few grindings of pepper, and serve at once.

1 pound (1 pint) fresh bay scallops or frozen scallops, thoroughly defrosted
8 tablespoons butter, cut into ½-inch bits
1 cup flour
1 teaspoon finely chopped garlic
3 tablespoons finely chopped fresh parsley
¼ teaspoon salt
Freshly ground black pepper

Tiny, tender, sautéed bay scallops are laced, Portuguese-style, with garlic and parsley, and served along with piping hot baked, stuffed tomatoes.

V

The Cranberry, a Bittersweet Treat

Fresh cranberries bring color and piquance to four sweets: cranberry ice *(left)*, sugar-frosted candied cranberries *(top)*, cranberry-orange sherbet *(right)* and cranberry chiffon pie *(bottom)*. In the 19th Century, the crimson of the fruit was captured in cranberry glass dishes like the old sugar castor in the foreground.

Among the agreeable things that the settlers of New England found in their new land were the bright red berries—cranberries—growing in dampish places along the shore. The Indians called them *sassamanesh* and ate them both raw and cooked. They pounded them with dried meat in a mortar and combined the resulting mixture with melted animal fat. This was pemmican, a long-keeping food that supplied concentrated nutrients. The Indians knew nothing about vitamins, of course, but they may have realized that the cranberries in their pemmican helped to keep them healthy through the winter. They also used cranberries as medicine, pounding them into a pulp that was spread on wounds to "draw the poison out." So far as I know, this bit of Indian folk medicine has never been corroborated by modern science, but perhaps there is something to it.

Cranberries may have been served at the Pilgrims' first Thanksgiving dinner, which took place in 1621 in October, a month when the berries are ripe. The Pilgrims probably had little or no sugar, but they would not have objected very much to the tartness of sugarless cranberry sauce. People in those days ate lots of acid things and apparently liked them. But cranberries do benefit from adding sugar, so when the New Englanders established trade with the West Indies and brought back sugar in exchange for their salt fish, they began to appreciate fully the gay and flavorsome but sour berries that offered themselves for the picking and kept fresh all winter. Ever since then cranberries have played an important part in the New England cuisine. They are almost a symbol of it.

Now that sugar is plentiful, the acidity of cranberries, far from being a fault, is their greatest culinary asset. Sweet fruits are common but extreme acidity combined with a pleasant, distinctive flavor is a rather rare combination. Cranberries can be cooked with a great deal of sugar and still not become too sweet. They wake up sweet desserts, enliven the blandness of apple cider or prune juice, and make wonderful sweet-sour relishes. When cut in quarters and distributed through a cake, they supply a delightful accent of tartness.

I admit a prejudice in favor of cranberries. As a native of Cape Cod, I was brought up in the region where cranberries were first domesticated, and now, with the help of a competent manager, I operate cranberry bogs for a family trust. There is no more pleasant kind of agriculture. Cranberry bogs (it will appear presently why they are called bogs) do not have to be replanted every year, or every 10 or 20 years. If properly cared for they bear indefinitely: some of ours are 100 years old and still going strong. Except for cleaning ditches, admittedly a nasty job, most of the heavy work is done by machines developed by ingenious Yankees for that specific purpose. Harvesting is a good-natured and picturesque festival, done mostly by local people who are decently paid.

A good many summer visitors came to Cape Cod from alien parts, such as Texas or Ohio, thinking cranberries grew on bushes like raspberries or blueberries. They could not be more wrong. In stature cranberries are among the lowest fruits that grow, as low even as strawberries. The cranberry plant is a recumbent vine that sends slender runners trailing close to the ground. From the runners spring short uprights set with narrowly oval leaves half an inch long. After the plants have been growing for a few years they cover the ground with a tangled mat of runners and uprights six or eight inches long and as springy as a horsehair mattress. It is nice to lie on of a summer afternoon, but cranberry growers discourage this recreation.

Wild cranberry vines are not very different from cultivated ones. If cranberries were really served at that first Thanksgiving dinner, the Pilgrims probably found them growing among sand dunes close to the roaring surf. Dunes are restless things that move like great slow waves. The wind blows away the sand between them until the surface is close to the water table. There the particles of sand are moist and cannot blow any more, so a flat area of bare white sand develops.

This is the promised land of the cranberry plant, which does not object in the least to salt sprayed ashore by the surf and demands little nourishment except light and an abundance of water. Gradually the plant takes possession of the bare sand (the seeds presumably are dropped by birds) and builds up its dense mat of vines.

The dune land owned by my family at East Sandwich on Cape Cod has several of these natural bogs, and they must look very much like those where the Pilgrims found their cranberries. They are beautiful in an unobtrusive way. In fall they turn first red, then a deep maroon. In spring they are tender green against the white sand, and in late June or early July small pink flowers appear on the ends of the uprights. While still in bud the flowers turn downward and have a fanciful resemblance to the heads of cranes. This is supposed by some to be the origin of the word cranberry, but I for one doubt it. The flowers are pretty (cranberries, after all, are related to azaleas and rhododendrons), but they are very small and bloom in out-of-the-way places. Not many people would be likely to associate their inconspicuous buds with the conspicuous red berries that ripen four months later. I suspect that "cranberry" is the English form of an ancient forgotten name for one of the cranberry's small European relatives, of which there are several, among them the famous lingonberry of Sweden.

A natural cranberry bog among the dunes is (unlike a domesticated one on higher ground) impermanent and likely to be overwhelmed at any time by a slowly advancing wave of sand. Even if this does not happen, the vines have their domain to themselves for only a limited number of years. Few plants thrive as well in clean, damp beach sand, but little by little soil of a sort accumulates among the vines, and other plants take root in it. Sedges and marsh grasses grow into great bunches that crowd ever closer together. Bushes appear, then trees. Before long they shade out the low cranberry vines, which retreat to the edge of the deepening thicket.

But they do not disappear from all the dune land, for the waves of sand are forever moving, exposing favorable bare places for the plants to colonize. One of our natural bogs is in the last stage of this cycle, about to be overwhelmed by tall bushes and pine trees, but not far away the cycle is beginning all over again. On a flat damp place newly swept bare by the wind a few young cranberry plants are hopefully spreading their runners across the virgin sand.

Wild cranberry vines, whether growing among sand dunes or in other damp places, do not normally bear large crops, so as the population of New England increased and the demand for cranberries grew, many Cape Codders tried to cultivate them. Some of the pioneers did no more than pluck competing vegetation out of the natural bogs, but about 1816 one Henry Hall of Dennis on Cape Cod noticed that the wind had blown sand over a mat of wild cranberry vines. Far from being discouraged, the vines grew more vigorously and bore an excellent crop. So he covered vines of his own with sand and got the same happy result.

Commercial cranberry cultivation dates from Hall's discovery. Present-day growers still sand their bogs about once in five years. They get better crops by doing so, but there is some disagreement about how the sanding works. Some think its chief effect is to discourage weeds and to bury dead leaves and vines so they will decay and release their nutrients. Others think the sand helps by reflecting sunlight onto the leaves. I favor an alternate theory: that the sanding encourages the old vines to root all along their length, thus renewing the bog by adding many thousands of young and vigorous plants per acre.

Many other tricks were required to domesticate the cranberry vine and make it produce heavy crops, and it took a century to discover them all. The vines can be transplanted to rich garden soil. There they grow luxuriantly, but they bear few berries and the first dry spell kills them. They will also grow in soggy swamps—and not bear well there either. What they like best is peat or a mixture of peat and sand covered by a layer of

Continued on page 118

115

In June, delicate flowers blossom in the bogs.

The bright berries are hard and ripe three months later.

The Tart Little Berries from the Bogs Along Massachusetts' Shores

The taste and color of cranberries—shown here in various stages of cultivation and harvesting—brightened many a simple Pilgrim meal. "The Indians and English use them much," wrote John Josselyn, who visited New England in 1663, "boyling them with Sugar for Sauce to eat with their Meat, and it is a delicate Sauce." Later, colonial ships carried barrels of cranberries on long voyages as a scurvy preventive for the crews. In the early 19th Century the berries were a delicacy in the capitals of Europe, and jars of "Cape Cod Bell Cranberry" sold for four shillings on the Strand in London. Yet the berries, part of the Thanksgiving tradition, have only recently come into everyday use throughout America. Cranberry juice, which New Englanders have been enjoying for 350 years, was not marketed nationwide until 1967. Now all sorts of processed sauces, relishes, juices and jellies are becoming available, and more and more cooks are using fresh cranberries—which are still grown in the bogs of Massachusetts, where the Pilgrims first found them. The pictures on these pages were taken at the author's place at East Sandwich.

116

A hand scoop is the best harvester for edges of the bog.

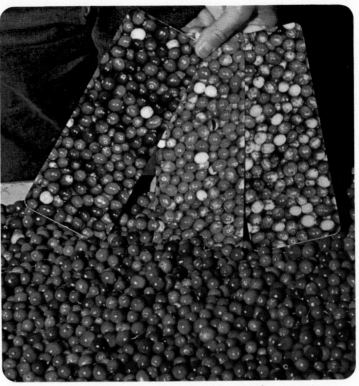

These berries match the top-grade card at left—a perfect crop.

Author Jonathan Leonard, at center, looks over his Cape Cod harvest of freshly picked cranberries packed in 35-pound crates.

pure sand. This is what they find in their natural homeland between the sand dunes, where peaty soil is common near the water table.

Even when they are given the peat and sand that they demand, cranberry vines do not bear well unless water conditions are controlled to their liking. During the growing season the water should stand 12 to 18 inches below the surface of the ground. This permits the cranberry roots, which die without air, to penetrate down to the peat. In wintertime the bog should be flooded ("flowed" is the local word) with water to protect the vines from extreme cold. The frozen cranberry bogs, incidentally, make fine, safe ice-skating rinks.

Meeting these finicky tastes is not easy. A well-built bog calls for skilled engineering, and it costs, at present prices, something like $5,000 per acre to establish. The starting point is usually a peat swamp or an arm of salt marsh that can be diked away from the tide. There should also be a reservoir or some other plentiful source of fresh water for winter flowing. All the surface vegetation is removed and a grid of ditches is dug to control the level of the soil water. Then the peat is covered with four or five inches of clean sand. Chopped cranberry vines are spread out on the sand and forced into it with a specially designed harrow. They readily take root and, if all goes well, grow into a mat of vines that bears full crops of berries four years after planting.

The best New England bogs, most of which are in Plymouth County just west of Cape Cod, are virtually weedless. Our own bogs are not, and although we are battling the weeds and getting the worst ones under control, I have a sneaking liking for them. They make the bogs look more natural, more in harmony with the seaside country around them.

Old, established cranberry bogs that have reached a kind of equilibrium with their surroundings are wonderfully varied and beautiful. All sorts of rare wildflowers bloom on or around them. Among the vines themselves bloom delicate pink orchids *(Pogonia, Arethusa* and *Calopogon)*. In the ditches grow white arrowleaf and the blazing four-foot spikes of scarlet cardinal flower. The pools are frosted with water lilies, both the usual white ones and the pink ones so common on Cape Cod. In the swamps and on the uplands around the bog crowd dozens of other flowers each in its place, each in its season: lady's-slippers, wild iris, luthrum, swamp azalea, joe-pye weed, steeple bush, fringed gentian, sweet pepper bush. My Norwegian niece, who loves wildflowers, calls the bog "the big flower garden."

I had always known that cranberry bogs are unusually rich in flowers, but I did not realize until recently why this is so. Most cultivated crops are alien species imported from far away and planted on artificial deserts kept bare of other plants. Cranberries are natives, and they grow in harmony with all their natural associates. The bogs themselves, the ditches and the borders around the bogs, which are kept clear of bushes and trees to promote air circulation, provide favorable growing conditions for all the moisture-loving flowers of New England from tiny violets and bluets in early spring to asters and goldenrod in late fall. Even after the cranberries are harvested, the graceful white seed-plumes of the grasses and sedges remain, swaying in the winter wind.

Besides being a flower garden, a cranberry bog is a natural zoo. Muskrats swim in the deeper ditches. (The cranberry grower wishes they did not, for they sometimes drill holes through the dikes.) Every shallow bit of water swarms with frogs and minor fish, some of which are big enough for small boys to covet. Pheasants and quail love the mowed margins where they find edible berries and seeds and nearby bushes to hide in. Wild mallard ducks cruise two by two in our widest ditch, which was once a tidal channel, and build their nests in a swamp nearby. I have never seen the nests, but in due season each pair is followed by a procession of fluffy ducklings.

More dramatic are the Canada geese, a pair of which (I hope it is the same pair) for several seasons has spent late May in a pool below one of our dikes. One of them always stands on the dike to keep sharp watch while the other feeds on water plants. After a while the watch-goose gives a gentle honk and waddles down to feed while its mate climbs up on the dike to take its turn at sentry duty. About June they depart, presumably to nest in Arctic Canada.

The senior citizen of the bog I see only once or twice a season: an enormous snapping turtle as big as a washtub and as dignified as an archbishop. He (or perhaps she) crawls out on a ditch bank and stares at me unblinking with antediluvian eyes. I know he has designs on those baby mallards, but I have not the heart to shoot him. He is probably older than I, and in a sense he is the owner of his part of the bog, so I leave him alone. He is welcome to the frogs, which are always in oversupply, and perhaps he catches some of those pesky muskrats too.

During the summer the bogs are kept mowed to discourage weeds, and two or three times a year they are sprayed by helicopter, using an insecticide that disintegrates in a few days. In June I rent 15 hives of bees and have them set at strategic places to pollinate the flowers. That is about all I can do. Passively I watch the berries grow from pinhead size, turn apple green, then whitish.

At last in August sparks of brilliant red begin to appear among the vines. The first berries, the Early Blacks, ripen in September, but the other popular variety, the Late Howes, may not be ripe until the end of October. Picking formerly was done with scoops, comblike devices with long wooden teeth that rake the berries off the vines. Scoops are still used to glean near the ditches, and to work one of them all day is a very athletic accomplishment. Most modern bogs are picked by gasoline-powered machines that push steel teeth through the vines and lift the berries by conveyor belt into a box or burlap bag. The bags are carried "ashore" on light, three-wheeled gas-powered trucks that are led with handles like children's wagons.

All this discussion about the charms of cranberry growing has little directly to do with cooking, so perhaps it should not get so much space and attention in a food book. But I wanted to expose readers to some of the reasons why traditional New Englanders have such sentimental feelings about cranberries. The berries are beautiful in themselves; the vines that produce them are beautiful, and they grow in beautiful places surrounded by the same kinds of living things that were their associates in ages past.

They are as natural on the shore as the surf or the wind from the sea.

When I was a boy I sometimes picked cranberries with an old-fashioned scoop and at the end of the bone-weary day took a few of the berries home. They were greeted with joy and made at once into the old-fashioned kind of cranberry sauce, merely cooked with sugar and water until the berries had burst. How good it was—the new crop! How it lit up a roast, or even a humble meat loaf.

There was always controversy in my family about cranberry sauce. Some of us liked it best with the skins and seeds strained out and cooled long enough to turn to a firm jelly. Some preferred it rather sour, others very sweet. For family occasions we made a special kind of sauce; each berry was painstakingly pricked with a needle so the air inside it could escape without bursting the skin. If these were cooked ever so carefully, they came to the table whole and very decorative.

Cranberry sauce is the most traditional cranberry dish, but it is only the beginning of the many delicious things that can be made with cranberries. My wife prefers cranberry relish made by grinding whole cranberries and quartered oranges coarsely in a meat grinder and combining them with sugar. The proportions can vary according to individual taste, but we think four cups of cranberries to one large orange and one cup of sugar is about right. No cooking is necessary. The relish keeps a long time in the refrigerator, and it is better after it has sat around for a few days. For a

Most Massachusetts cranberries are harvested dry, but on some bogs that are level enough, water harvesting has been introduced. Mechanical pickers called egg beaters churn their way through the flooded bog, stirring the water and knocking the berries from the vines. The berries are then swept ashore with a boom.

different cranberry relish apples are used, or apples and oranges. In each case the cranberries provide both flavor and the needed acidity.

Every Cape Cod family has its favorite recipe for cranberry bread (really a semisweet cake) and often for cranberry muffins *(Recipe Index)*. Cranberry pie is great to eat, and so is apple pie enlivened with cranberries. Chopped fresh cranberries add color and stimulating flavor to almost any kind of salad or cole slaw. Cranberry juice is fine in fruit punches, and with vodka it makes a beautiful cocktail. Very sneaky, though; you hardly know the vodka is there.

Cranberry desserts are innumerable, ranging from gelatins and sherbets to cranberry tapioca, cranberry rice pudding and cranberry steamed pudding. My own favorite is my wife's cranberry "goodin puddin'," which is a delectable pielike thing with no bottom crust and a browned, cakelike covering. Most guests whom we honor with it ask spontaneously for the recipe; there is a version of it in this book called Upside Down Cranberry Pudding *(Recipe Index)*.

Cranberry dishes go on forever. Ocean Spray Cranberries Inc., the grower-owned cooperative that markets most of the Cape's cranberries, publishes a book of 101 of them; many more can be found by a little searching, and any good cook can invent cranberry dishes of her own. All she need remember is that where there is sugar around, the cranberry's flavorsome acidity is almost always welcome.

Upside-down Cranberry Pudding

Preheat the oven to 325°. With a pastry brush, spread the 2 tablespoons of softened butter over the bottom and sides of an 8-inch pie tin. Wash the cranberries and pat them dry. Spread them evenly in the bottom of the buttered pan and sprinkle the berries with the chopped walnuts and ⅓ cup of the sugar.

In a mixing bowl, beat the egg and the remaining ½ cup of sugar together with a wire whisk or a rotary or electric beater, until the mixture thickens and clings to the beater. Beating constantly, add the flour, a few tablespoonfuls at a time. Then beat in the melted cooled butter and pour the batter over the cranberries and nuts. Bake in the middle of the oven for 45 minutes, or until the top is golden brown and a cake tester inserted in the center comes out clean. Cool the pudding to room temperature.

Meanwhile, in a chilled bowl, whip the cream with a whisk or a rotary or electric beater until it is stiff enough to stand in unwavering peaks on the beater when it is lifted from the bowl. Refrigerate covered with plastic wrap until ready to serve.

To unmold and serve the pudding, run a thin-bladed knife around the sides of the pan to loosen it. Place an inverted serving plate over the pudding and, grasping plate and pan together firmly, carefully turn them over. The pudding should slide out easily. Decorate the pudding as fancifully as you like by piping the whipped cream onto the top through a pastry bag fitted with a decorative tube, or simply spread the cream over the pudding and swirl it about with a small spatula.

To serve 6

2 tablespoons butter, softened, plus 6 tablespoons butter, melted and cooled
1½ cups firm fresh unblemished cranberries
¼ cup coarsely chopped walnuts
⅓ cup plus ½ cup sugar
1 egg
½ cup flour
½ cup heavy cream, chilled

Cranberry Nut Pie

Following the directions for the short-crust pastry dough for a lattice-topped pie in the Recipe Booklet, roll out half of the pastry dough and fit it into a 9-inch pie tin. Refrigerate the pie shell and the remaining dough while you prepare the filling.

Preheat the oven to 400°. Wash the cranberries under cold running water and pat them completely dry with paper towels. Then put the berries through the coarsest blade of a food grinder into a deep bowl. Combine the cranberries, walnuts, sugar, flour, raisins, orange juice, orange peel, melted butter and salt. Stir until well mixed, then spoon the filling into the chilled pie shell, spreading it and smoothing the top with a spatula. Roll out the remaining pastry dough and cut it into ½-inch-wide lattice strips. Place the strips on top of the pie, first coating them with the egg yolk-and-milk mixture as described in the directions for a lattice-top pie in the Recipe Booklet.

Bake the pie in the middle of the oven for about 1 hour, or until the pastry is golden brown. (Check from time to time and if the edge of the pie begins to brown too quickly, cover it loosely with a strip of foil.)

Serve the pie hot, or cooled to room temperature, accompanied if you like by unsweetened whipped cream or vanilla ice cream.

To make a 9-inch pie

Short-crust pastry dough for a lattice-topped pie (*Recipe Booklet*)
3½ cups firm fresh unblemished cranberries
⅓ cup coarsely chopped walnuts
1 cup sugar
4 teaspoons flour
½ cup seedless raisins
¼ cup strained fresh orange juice
1 teaspoon finely grated orange peel
3 tablespoons butter, melted
⅛ teaspoon salt
1 egg yolk beaten with 1 tablespoon milk

Cranberry-nut pie is an aromatic delectation, crowded with berries, walnuts, raisins and orange peel, and flaunting a fluted lattice crust.

To make about 5 cups

1 pound (4 cups) firm fresh
    unblemished cranberries
2 large thin-skinned oranges,
    preferably a seedless variety
2 cups sugar

Uncooked Cranberry-Orange Relish

Wash the cranberries under cold running water and pat them dry with paper towels. Cut the oranges into quarters. (If the oranges have seeds, pick them out with the tip of a knife.) Then put the cranberries and the orange quarters (skins and all) through the coarsest blade of a food grinder into a deep glass or ceramic bowl. Add the sugar and mix well with a wooden spoon. Taste and add more sugar if desired.

Cover with plastic wrap and let the relish stand at room temperature for about 24 hours to develop flavor before serving. (Tightly covered, the relish can safely be refrigerated for 2 to 3 weeks.)

To make a dozen 2½-inch muffins

1 tablespoon butter, softened, plus 4
    tablespoons butter, melted and
    cooled
1 cup firm fresh unblemished
    cranberries
2¾ cups flour
¾ cup sugar
4 teaspoons double-acting baking
    powder
½ teaspoon salt
1 cup milk
1 egg, lightly beaten

Cranberry Muffins

Preheat the oven to 400°. With a pastry brush, spread the softened butter over the inside surfaces of a medium-sized 12-cup muffin tin (each cup should be about 2½ inches across at the top).

Wash the cranberries under cold running water and pat the berries dry with paper towels. Put them through the coarsest blade of a food grinder into a glass or ceramic bowl and set aside.

Combine the flour, sugar, baking powder and salt and sift into a deep mixing bowl. Stirring constantly with a large spoon, pour in the milk in a thin stream. When the milk is completely absorbed, stir in the egg and the 4 tablespoons of melted butter. Add the ground cranberries and continue to stir until all the ingredients are well combined.

Ladle about ⅓ cup of the batter into each of the muffin-tin cups, filling them about ⅔ full. Bake in the middle of the oven for 30 minutes, or until the muffins are puffed and brown on top, and a cake tester or toothpick inserted in the center comes out clean. Run a knife around the inside of each cup to loosen the muffins, then turn them out of the tin and serve at once, or cool to room temperature before serving.

To make about 1 quart

2 cups (½ pound) firm fresh
    unblemished cranberries
4 cups water
1½ cups sugar
1 teaspoon lemon juice

Cranberry Ice

Wash the cranberries under cold running water. Combine them and the water in a 2- to 3-quart enameled or stainless-steel saucepan and bring to a boil over high heat. Reduce the heat to low, cover tightly and simmer for 10 to 12 minutes, or until they can be easily mashed against the side of the pan with a spoon.

Purée the cranberries with their cooking liquid through a food mill into a glass or ceramic bowl. Or rub them through a fine sieve with the back of a spoon, pressing down hard on the skins before discarding them. Stir in the sugar and lemon juice.

Pour the mixture into 2 ice-cube trays from which the dividers have been removed. Then freeze the cranberry ice for 3 to 4 hours, stirring and mashing it every 30 minutes or so with a fork to break up the solid particles that will form on the bottom and sides of the trays. The finished ice should have a fine, snowy texture.

To serve, spoon the ice into parfait glasses or dessert dishes.

124

A hot cranberry muffin, split in half, with dollops of butter, waits tantalizingly on a child's tin plate, a treat for any time of day.

VI

A Talent for Pies and Preserves

Pies, contrary to popular belief, were not invented in North America. Probably every bread making people of the Old World used dough as a container in which to bake fruit or other food and so make their bread more interesting. Those venison pasties that Robin Hood fed to his merry men were pies of a sort, and the prologue to the Cook's tale in Chaucer's *The Canterbury Tales* tells of an unethical pie dealer who was notorious for selling pasties "That hath been twies hoot and twies coold."

Nevertheless pies have come to be a northeast American specialty. The brick ovens of colonial times were rated in terms of pies; there were 10-pie and even 20-pie ovens. Pies were eaten at every meal including breakfast, a pleasant custom that still persists among men who control the food their households serve. Though often deplored by the diet conscious, nothing could be more fitting. An apple or cherry pie is far fuller of calories than the orange juice and buttered toast that is the standard breakfast of modern urban man, but is much better eating.

In the old days, especially on farms and especially in winter, pies were turned out by mass production. Enough for a week were routinely baked and put aside in a cold closet or unheated back room. Some housewives baked 100 pies at a time, froze them out in the snow (which did them no harm) and then thawed and warmed them for each meal in front of the fire blazing on the hearth. Pies went into the woods with logging crews and put out to sea on sailing ships as last, loving offerings of relatives ashore. They served innumerable occasions. Nothing is more convenient than a substantial, two-crust pie. It can be eaten hot or cold, and no

A rhubarb and lemon-cream pie and two bowls of fresh rhubarb, baked with brown sugar, cool in the window of a Connecticut kitchen. The whole nutmegs on the sill symbolize Connecticut's nickname, the Nutmeg State. It got the name not because it grows nutmeg, a tropical spice, but because its early inhabitants had a reputation of being canny about making and selling fake, wooden ones.

implement is needed but some sort of knife to cut it into handy segments.

Apple pie is the standard, archetypical pie; there are dozens of ways to make it, most, but not all of them good. The simplest apple pies contain nothing but apples and sugar; if the apples are solid, tart cooking apples and the crust is plain but properly made, they are excellent fare, even for children, who take to them eagerly. They can also be much more elaborate. Here is Mrs. Silvester Gardiner telling how a superlative apple pie was supposed to be baked in Boston in 1763: "After having made a good puff-paste Crust, lay fome round the Sides of the Dish. Pare, quarter, and core your apples & then lay a Row of Apples as close and thick as you can in your Dish; upon which throw in half the quantity of Sugar you intend for your Pye; then throw in a little Lemon Peel minced fine, over that again and over your Sugar and Apples a little Lemon; then put a Clove here and there, then put in the rest of Your Apples, and over them the rest of your Sugar, and over all fqueeze a little more Lemon. Boil the peelings an the Cores of your Apples in foft Water, with a blade of Mace untill it is rich; then ftrain it and boil the ftrained Liquor or Syrup with a little Sugar, till there is but little of it left, and that very rich and good, which pour into your Pie, then cover and bake. . . . In the same way you make a Pear Pie."

Among the treasured recipes of New England households are dozens of other kinds of apple pie. Some of them call for thin-sliced instead of quartered apples, some even for applesauce (I do not admire this). Some include butter in the filling (I do admire this) or even tiny cubes of salt pork. The most popular spices used are cinnamon and nutmeg, which should be administered sparingly. A bit of lemon juice may be added.

In colonial New England apples were the most common fruit in pie; they were cheap and plentiful, as they still are. They keep through the winter and can be dried for use at any time of year. Their only failing is a tendency to blandness, especially after long storage. This is why slightly sour green apples make the best pies and also why Mrs. Gardiner used lemon juice. Green apples and lemons were not always available in her day, so cooks turned to other acid fruits to add variety and impact to their apple pies. Sour cherries, blackberries and rhubarb add balance, or a small quantity of cut-up, fresh cranberries adds welcome color and tartness. Cranberries, of course, can also stand on their own in a pie. Combined with egg white, gelatin and heavy cream they make a delicious cranberry chiffon pie; with walnuts, raisins and orange rind they make a spicy cranberry nut pie *(both, Recipe Index)*.

My own family never turned out pies in large lots, but pie-making nevertheless was a ritual of interest to us hungry children. More crust was rolled than was needed for the scheduled pies, so some of the excess was made into turnovers filled with jelly, marmalade and peanut butter, or anything else within reason that we suggested. If any crust was still left over it was cut in narrow strips, sprinkled with sugar and cinnamon, baked and fed to us, hot from the oven. We considered them our special perquisite and so professed to like them even more than the pies.

Cherry pie was never as important in New England as in other parts of the United States. Yankees prefer blueberry pie, which, when properly baked, is a glorious thing. Unfortunately it is often made badly. Restaurant and store-bought blueberry pies usually have more flour or cornstarch in them than blueberries, and many home-baked blueberry pies are too runny.

Wild blueberries are best for pies. Picking them is still a considerable industry in Maine, where great areas of barren land are covered with low bushes that in season are covered with small, somewhat acid berries. In the rest of New England the bushes do best on burned-over forest land. This was the ravaged condition of much of Cape Cod's interior when I was a boy. Sometimes I picked as many as 20 quarts a day, which I divided between my family, gratis, and the grocery store across Main Street from our house, at 20 cents a quart. Modern fire-fighting equipment douses most forest fires while they are still small, making the woods tall and beautiful—but the low-growing blueberry bushes have been shaded out. The large cultivated blueberries that grow on big bushes in marshy areas are apt to be too sweet to make perfect pies. Yet even the sweetest can be remedied with a touch of lemon juice.

Most blueberries are so juicy that when they are used as filling they drain out of the pie as soon as it is cut and have to be collected with a spoon. The way to fix this defect is to toss the berries around with a very little flour, perhaps a tablespoon for a quart. The flour thickens the juice just enough to keep it from being too runny. For children blueberry pie has an additional advantage—it stains the teeth, which they enjoy.

The splendid taste of a good mincemeat pie is made possible by the great variety of its ingredients. At left, from top to bottom: beef brisket, beef tongue and nutmeg. In front of the slice of pie: raisins, chopped citron, and suet. In front of the crock: lemon, grated lemon peel, figs, currants, candied orange and lemon peel and cinnamon. At right, next to bottles of brandy and sherry, is a bowl of mincemeat.

The king pie of all is, or was, mince pie *(Recipe Index)*. I say "was" advisedly, because modern mince pie is usually filled with little more than raisins and goo. Proper mince pie contains mincemeat, an elaborate, rib-filling compound based on real meat, usually beef though other meats may be added. Its origins go back to Europe where, centuries ago, the discovery was made that the surplus meat of autumn would keep indefinitely if mixed with sugar or sugar-containing ingredients. The reason, which people in those days did not know, is that spoilage bacteria cannot live in a strong sugar solution.

In my family's house the annual making of mincemeat, presided over by my Aunt Alice, was an exciting rite, rich in creative tasks for children. My aunt boiled the tough, lean beef and freed it of gristle and other unwanted parts. Then we children chopped it fine in wooden chopping bowls. My mother maintained that grinding it with a meat grinder was just as good, but Aunt Alice, a traditionalist, would have none of such modernities. We also chopped suet, after freeing it of papery membranes. We trimmed and chopped small piles of figs and raisins, citron and candied orange and lemon peel. All this took a long time, but we had two chopping bowls and two choppers, so the task was sociable. When everything was chopped sufficiently fine, my aunt added sugar and boiled cider. I have not seen this last ingredient for many years, in or out of mincemeat. It was apple cider boiled down to a heavy syrup. It did not taste very good by itself, but was part of the mince pie tradition. I think

it dates from remote times when apple juice was a cheap source of sugar.

The ingredients were simmered for an hour or two with spices tied up in a cheesecloth: cinnamon, allspice, nutmeg and cloves. As the big, fragrant kettleful cooled, it was stirred occasionally to keep melted suet from collecting on the surface, and when it was barely warm several cups of cognac were stirred into it. I remember some discussion about that: none of my family were prohibitionists, but certain neighbors were, so it was agreed not to advertise the brandy in our mincemeat.

When the mincemeat was finished, it was packed into a big stone crock with a stone cover and taken down cellar. We children would have liked to eat it cold with spoons for breakfast, dinner and supper, but it was reserved for pies and pies alone.

Not everyone made mincemeat in this full, old-fashioned way. Some households used less meat or none at all. Others omitted the suet. Sometimes ground spices were added without use of the cheesecloth bag, which made the mincemeat dark. But everywhere mincemeat was considered important. My father told of one old lady who made pies in quantity and insisted that half of them must be mince. To distinguish between the two varieties, she marked the mince pies "T.M." on the crust for " 'tis mince." The others she marked "T.M." for " 'tain't mince."

There are other ways besides pies to effect the desirable bread-and-fruit combination with considerably less effort. A family dessert that I always liked was made by buttering half-slices of white bread (preferably stale) and building them up in a baking dish with alternate layers of sliced apples and a judicious sprinkling of water and sugar. The top layer of bread was buttered extra thick. When the dish was baked, the liquids saturated the lower bread slices. The layer on top was saturated only on the underside. Its upper surface turned golden brown and was the prize part of the dish. We called this concoction apple bread pudding. Blueberries, peaches, pears or raspberries can be used instead of apples.

One fine old-fashioned fruit dish has a picturesque name—grunt—that attracts some people but repels others. Blueberry grunt *(Recipe Index)* is the commonest kind, and to cook it is simple indeed. Just stew the berries with sugar and a little water until they are soft, which takes about five minutes. While they are still boiling drop spoonfuls of biscuit dough into them. Then simmer until the biscuits are well cooked through and have a dumplinglike texture. Ladle blueberries over the biscuits before serving. Grunt can be made with other kinds of berries or fruits, and it tastes much better than it sounds. Perhaps a change of name would help, but the alternate New England name—slump—does not help much.

A closely related dish is pandowdy *(Recipe Index)* nowadays sometimes called cobbler—not to be confused with the old New England sherry-based drink. Pandowdy is made by arranging cut-up apples in a shallow pan, sprinkling them with sugar, a little cinnamon, nutmeg and cloves, dotting them with butter and covering them with biscuit dough molded to fit the pan. The whole thing is baked until the crust is done.

Pandowdy (or cobbler) can also be made with blueberries or other suitable fruit, but perhaps the best way to cook blueberries is in blueberry cake, which is more like pudding than cake. It is made by baking a generous layer of blueberries between two layers of rich, sweet batter. It is served hot, and if its own berries do not make it juicy enough, additional stewed blueberries can be poured over it. To make blueberry cake (or bread) that can be eaten gracefully with the fingers, the berries must be used sparingly to keep their juiciness under control, and the batter must be stiff enough to prevent them from sinking to the bottom. A trick that helps keep the berries well-distributed is to shake them in a paper bag with a little flour.

The old-time New Englanders who were such great pie makers were also great picklers. In this case climate was the mother of invention. As the growing season gets shorter and the winter longer, people are forced to develop better ways to keep their foodstuffs through the long unproductive season. Some preserved foods are so good that they are admired for themselves, not merely as ways to prolong the life of perishables.

Pickles are a good example of a creative preserving method. They started out as a way of making cucumbers, cabbages and other vegetables last through the winter by encouraging them to ferment in brine and generate so much lactic acid that spoilage bacteria could not grow. This method is still used in some places, to make sauerkraut for instance, but it was never very popular in New England or eastern Canada where apples were plentiful. If you squeeze the juice out of apples, you get sweet cider. If you leave this alone for a while, yeast fermentation turns its sugar into alcohol and you have hard cider, the common alcoholic drink of colonial times. Hard cider will keep indefinitely if corked tight in a bottle or barrel, but if air gets to it, another kind of fermentation (bacterial this time) turns its alcohol to acetic acid. What you have now is cider vinegar that will acidify and preserve almost anything. No need to bother with slow and uncertain lactic fermentation.

New Englanders made pickling a test of their ingenuity. Besides such ordinary things as cucumbers, they pickled mushrooms, onions, tomatoes, beets, string beans, green walnuts—even nasturtium seeds. Some of these foods they pickled plain, the idea being to soak them later in water, remove most of their salt and acidity and cook them as if fresh. Other foods they enlivened in subtle ways, and these are the pickles that have survived efficient modern methods of canning and freezing vegetables.

The traditional pickles I like best are sweet mixed pickles (Recipe Index) made of chunks of nearly everything the garden provides, including cauliflower, tomatoes, cucumbers, onions and sometimes peppers. Another favorite is mustard pickle, made with the same variety of vegetables, and I like it with lots of mustard, not just enough to make it mustard-colored. Then, of course, there is the inevitable green tomato relish (Recipe Index). When summer fades into autumn and the days grow cooler, the tomato plants in the garden do not get the message. They go right on producing until they are killed by the first frost. This leaves a lot of green tomatoes that will never ripen, and thrifty New England housewives try to smuggle them into every kind of pickle.

The best traditional New England pickle is made of watermelon rind. This may seem odd, since watermelons do not grow well in New England now and grew even worse in the past before short-season varieties

132   Continued on page 137

In the late spring, the beach-plum bushes along the New England shore bloom in a snowy profusion of delicate white petals.

Wild Fruits and Berries for Homemade Jellies

On sunny, breezy days with a hint of autumn in the air, New Englanders yearning for homemade jellies ramble for hours in search of the beach plums, rose hips and fox grapes that still grow wild in many places. Beach plums grow close to the shore, straggling across sand dunes or over brick walls, or forming thick bushes four or five feet high. As the small fruit ripens in September and October it turns from a pinkish to a deep purple *(right)*. Inside the tough and acrid skin, the flesh is juicy and sweet. To provide added pectin to help jelly or jam to set, some of the less ripe plums are picked along with the ripe.

On Martha's Vineyard a summer visitor, Nana Fletcher, picks rose hips from a cluster of Salt Spray rose bushes.

The Salt Spray rose, known to botanists as *Rosa rugosa,* was brought to America from China in the early 19th Century. After its pink-and-white flower dies, a bright red fruit forms, called a rose hip *(below).* It makes a tart jelly, and is a rich source of Vitamin C.

were developed. The key to the anomaly is the citron-melon, a relative of the watermelon raised especially for making sweet pickles. I have not seen a citron-melon for years, but I hear they are still grown in out-of-the-way places. They look like small round watermelons, but their inner flesh never gets red and edible. In recompense their rind, the part that goes into pickles, is extra thick. Thanks to the citron-melon, old New England had watermelon pickle without watermelons. Modern picklers use real watermelons imported from the South, but I notice that as they are improved as eating melons, their rind gets softer and thinner and less suited for pickling. Perhaps if this trend continues the old-time citron-melons will make a comeback on the pickle scene.

As a Cape Codder I cannot end this chapter without some mention of beach plums, which many readers have never heard of and most have never seen except as expensive jars of deep red jelly on roadside stands. They are small plums seldom more than half an inch long that grow wild on bushes near the sea, and they are the reason for the Plum Islands and Plum Beaches scattered along the northeastern coast. In spring the bushes are mounds of small white blossoms, but often the flowers do not set and no fruit is produced. In other years, for some reason, the bushes are thick with fruit. Once I picked three quarts of plums from a bush no bigger than half a Volkswagen; it had yielded not a single plum the year before.

When a good plum year is in prospect, both natives and summer people prowl the sandy roads mentally marking the best bushes, watching the competition, appraising the seriousness of "Keep Off" signs, and waiting for the earliest day when the beach plums will be ripe enough to pick. When that time comes, it seems as if every bush has its picker.

Beach plums are not eaten as fruit; they are too sour. Their talent is for making a wonderful, tangy jelly that has a remarkable flavor resembling nothing else. It is best when served with meat, and a touch of it can turn an ordinary roast into a super-roast. Beach-plum jelly brings handsome prices, but it is almost always scarce because the recalcitrant bushes have baffled all efforts to grow them commercially. Cultivation seems to offend them. When planted in rich, well-fertilized soil, they grow tall but produce hardly any fruit. Even when planted in the poor sandy soil that they seem to prefer, they sulk in captivity. Apparently they need the stress and adversity that is inseparable from life along the shore.

The most productive bushes I ever saw were less than a foot tall. They were growing in pure white beach sand on the forward side of an advancing sand dune—hardly a favorable environment—but the smallest twigs were loaded with large plums. I was interested in this phenomenon and found by a little digging that large bushes were buried in the sand below. Apparently they knew they were about to be overwhelmed, so they put every bit of remaining strength into producing plums whose hard, round seeds were their only hope of posterity. Just when I came to this conclusion I saw a task force of summer people approaching with empty baskets and plum-hungry eyes. So I hurriedly stripped plums from the heroic bush tops and put them in my pockets. On my way home from the dunes I planted them in sandy soil that I thought they would enjoy. I hope some of them sprouted and are still growing there.

Opposite: Three jellies homemade from wild fruit: beach plum *(top),* rose hip *(right)* and wild grape.

The wild fox grape, or *Vitis labrusca,* is the largest of the 20 species native to the United States, the only one producing black, red and white berries. The species has too little sugar to be used in wine making, but the black grapes *(below)* make fine jelly. The vines may extend 60 feet, looping over tree branches or winding through brush. This bunch was from a vine spreading over a covered bridge in Vermont.

Cranberry Sauce

Wash the cranberries in a colander under cold running water. Combine the berries with the sugar and water in a small, heavy enameled or stainless-steel saucepan and, stirring frequently, bring them to a boil over high heat. Then reduce the heat to low and, still stirring from time to time, simmer uncovered for 4 or 5 minutes, until the skins of the cranberries begin to pop and the berries are tender. Do not overcook them to the point where they become mushy.

Remove the pan from the heat and stir in the grated orange peel. With a rubber spatula, scrape the entire contents of the pan into a 2-cup mold or small bowl. Refrigerate for 2 or 3 hours until the sauce is thoroughly chilled and firm to the touch.

To unmold and serve the sauce, run a thin-bladed knife around the sides of the mold or bowl to loosen it and dip the bottom briefly in hot water. Place a serving plate upside down over the mold and, grasping plate and mold firmly together, invert them. The cranberry sauce should slide out of the mold easily.

To make about 1½ cups

2 cups (½ pound) firm fresh unblemished cranberries
1 cup sugar
½ cup water
1 teaspoon finely grated fresh orange peel

Blueberry Pancakes

Wash the blueberries in a colander under cold running water, discarding any stems or blemished berries. Spread the berries on paper towels and pat them completely dry.

Combine the flour, sugar, baking powder and salt and sift into a deep mixing bowl. Make a well in the center and pour in the eggs, milk and 2 tablespoons of the cooled melted butter. With a large spoon, gradually incorporate the dry ingredients into the liquid ones. Do not overmix; the pancakes will be lighter if the batter is not too smooth. Gently stir the blueberries into the batter, being careful not to crush them.

Warm a large, heavy griddle over moderate heat until a drop of water flicked onto it splutters and evaporates instantly. Grease the griddle lightly with a pastry brush dipped in the remaining 4 tablespoons of butter. Fry 3 or 4 pancakes at a time, leaving space between them so they can spread into 4-inch rounds. For each one, pour about ¼ cup of the batter onto the griddle and fry for about 1 minute until small, scattered bubbles have formed—and begin to break—on the surface. Immediately turn the pancake with a wide metal spatula and cook for a minute until the other side is golden brown.

Stack the finished pancakes on a heated plate. Then repeat the procedure, brushing the griddle with melted butter when necessary, until all the blueberry pancakes are fried. Serve at once with butter and maple syrup or cinnamon sugar.

NOTE: To make apple pancakes, follow the same procedures and substitute 3 large tart cooking apples (peeled, quartered, cored and very thinly sliced) for the blueberries.

To make about 15 four-inch pancakes

1½ cups fresh ripe blueberries
2 cups flour
2 tablespoons sugar
4 teaspoons double-acting baking powder
½ teaspoon salt
2 eggs, lightly beaten
1¾ cups milk
6 tablespoons butter, melted and cooled

One recipe (above) does double duty to produce a pair of breakfast dishes as attractive as they are satisfying: blueberry pancakes and apple pancakes (shown with sausages). Simply switch from berries to apples.

To make one 9-inch pie

2 tablespoons butter plus 5
  tablespoons butter, softened and
  cut into ½-inch bits
1 pound firm fresh rhubarb,
  trimmed, washed and cut into
  ½-inch lengths (about 2 cups)
1¼ cups sugar
5 egg yolks
½ cup strained fresh lemon juice
2 teaspoons freshly grated lemon
  peel
1 teaspoon unflavored gelatin
2 tablespoons cold water
1 cup heavy cream, chilled
A 9-inch short-crust pastry shell,
  baked and cooled (Recipe
  Booklet)

Rhubarb and Lemon-Cream Pie

In a heavy 8- to 10-inch skillet, melt 2 tablespoons of the butter over moderate heat. When the foam begins to subside, add the rhubarb and stir in ¾ cup of the sugar. Cover tightly and steam the rhubarb for about 10 minutes, sliding the pan back and forth over the heat from time to time to roll the pieces around.

When the rhubarb is somewhat translucent and slightly tender, transfer the pieces gently with a slotted spoon to a fine sieve set over a bowl. Let the rhubarb drain without turning or disturbing the pieces, then set it aside to cool completely; return the drained liquid to the juices remaining in the skillet and reserve them.

Meanwhile, prepare the lemon curd in the following fashion: In a heavy 1½- to 2-quart enameled or stainless-steel saucepan, combine the butter bits, the remaining ½ cup of sugar, the egg yolks and lemon juice. Cook over the lowest possible heat, stirring constantly until the mixture thickens enough to heavily coat the back of a spoon. Do not let the lemon curd come anywhere near a boil or it will curdle. Pour the lemon curd into a small bowl, stir in the grated lemon peel and set aside to cool completely to room temperature.

In a heatproof measuring cup, sprinkle the gelatin over 2 tablespoons of cold water. When the gelatin has softened for 2 or 3 minutes, set the cup in a small pan of simmering water and cook over low heat, stirring constantly, until the gelatin dissolves completely. Remove the gelatin from the pan and let it cool to room temperature.

With a wire whisk or a rotary or electric beater, whip the cream in a large chilled bowl. When it begins to thicken, add the cooled but still fluid gelatin. Continue to whip until the cream is thick enough to stand in soft peaks on the beater when it is lifted from the bowl.

Stir ½ cup of the whipped cream into the lemon curd, then scoop the lemon mixture over the remaining cream and fold them gently but thoroughly together with a rubber spatula. Pour the lemon cream into the baked, cooled pastry shell, spreading it and smoothing the top with the spatula. Refrigerate until the filling is firm to the touch.

Bring the reserved rhubarb juice to a boil over high heat and, stirring occasionally, cook briskly until it is reduced to ½ cup. Strain the juice through a fine sieve into a bowl, and let it cool to room temperature. Then spread the reserved rhubarb evenly over the lemon-cream filling and brush the top of the pie with the strained juice glaze. Refrigerate the pie until ready to serve.

To make about 4 quarts

10 cups fresh corn kernels, cut from
  about 20 large ears of corn
4 cups finely chopped onions
1 cup finely chopped green bell
  peppers
1 cup finely chopped red bell
  peppers
2¼ cups (1 pound) tightly packed
  dark brown sugar
3 tablespoons celery seed
3 tablespoons dry mustard
3 tablespoons salt
1 quart cider vinegar

Corn Relish

Combine the corn, onions, green and red peppers, brown sugar, celery seed, mustard, salt and cider vinegar in a 6- to 8-quart enameled or stainless-steel casserole and mix well. Stirring the mixture occasionally, bring to a boil over high heat, then reduce the heat to low, partially cover the casserole and simmer for 15 minutes.

Immediately ladle the relish into hot sterilized jars, filling them to within ⅛ inch of the tops and following the directions for canning and sealing in the Recipe Booklet.

Baked Rhubarb

To serve 4

Preheat the oven to 350°. Combine the rhubarb and brown sugar in a heavy 3- to 4-quart enameled casserole and toss them about with a spoon until they are well mixed. Cover the casserole tightly and bake on the middle shelf of the oven for about 20 to 30 minutes, or until the rhubarb pieces are tender but still intact.

Ladle the baked rhubarb into four heated individual dessert bowls and present the cream separately in a pitcher. Serve at once.

2 pounds firm fresh rhubarb, trimmed, washed and cut into 1½-inch lengths (about 4 cups)
2 cups light brown sugar
1 cup heavy cream

Maine Sweet Pickles

To make about 5 quarts

Combine the tomatoes, cauliflower, cucumbers, onions and salt in a 10- to 12-quart enameled pot and pour in enough cold water to cover the vegetables by at least 2 inches. Stir until the salt dissolves, then place a lid on the pot and let the vegetables steep in the brine at room temperature for at least 12 hours.

Drain the brine from the vegetables and in its place add 4 cups of the vinegar and 2 quarts of cold water. Stirring gently, bring to a boil over high heat. Turn off the heat at once and, with a large slotted spoon, transfer the vegetables to a large glass or ceramic bowl. Pour off and discard the vinegar solution.

Pour the remaining 6 cups of vinegar into the pot. Add the brown sugar and pickling spice and bring to a boil over high heat, stirring until the sugar dissolves. Return the vegetables to the pot and cook over high heat. When bubbles begin to form around the edges of the pan again, and the vegetables are barely tender but still somewhat crisp to the bite, turn off the heat immediately.

With a large spoon, pack the vegetables tightly into hot sterilized jars. Ladle the hot liquid from the pot over the vegetables a little at a time, allowing it to flow through to the bottom of the jar before adding more. Fill the jars to within ⅛ inch of the top and follow the directions for canning and sealing in the Recipe Booklet.

10 medium-sized firm green tomatoes (about 3 pounds), washed, stemmed and cut into ¾-inch chunks (8 cups)
2 large firm cauliflowers (about 1½ pounds), trimmed, washed and cut into 1-inch flowerets (8 cups)
5 medium-sized cucumbers (about 2½ pounds), peeled and cut into ¾-inch chunks (8 cups)
6 medium-sized onions (about 2 pounds), peeled and cut into ¾-inch chunks (8 cups)
1 cup salt
10 cups cider vinegar
8 cups dark brown sugar
2 tablespoons mixed pickling spice

Green Tomato Relish

To make about 3 quarts

Spread the tomato slices in layers on a large, deep platter, sprinkling each layer with salt as you proceed and using ¼ cup salt in all. Cover the platter with foil or plastic wrap and set it aside at room temperature for at least 12 hours.

Pour off the liquid that has accumulated around the slices and transfer the tomatoes to a 5- to 6-quart enameled casserole. Add the onions, peppers, sugar, celery seed, dry mustard, cinnamon, allspice, cloves and the remaining 2 tablespoons of salt. Pour in the vinegar; it should cover the vegetables completely. If necessary add more. Stirring gently but constantly, bring the mixture to a boil over high heat. Reduce the heat to low and simmer partially covered for about 5 minutes, or until the vegetables are barely tender.

At once ladle the relish into hot sterilized jars, filling them to ⅛ inch of the tops and following the directions for canning and sealing given in the Recipe Booklet.

20 medium-sized firm green tomatoes (about 6 pounds), washed, stemmed, cut in half and cut crosswise into ½-inch-thick slices
¼ cup plus 2 tablespoons salt
6 medium-sized onions (about 2 pounds), peeled and cut crosswise into ¼-inch-thick slices
6 medium-sized red bell peppers, seeded, deribbed and cut lengthwise into ½-inch-wide strips
1 cup sugar
2 teaspoons celery seed
1 teaspoon dry mustard
1 teaspoon ground cinnamon
½ teaspoon ground allspice
¼ teaspoon ground cloves
4 to 6 cups cider vinegar

Homemade pickles and relishes like those shown here are canned in jars to preserve the summer's vegetables for wintertime eating. Dried pickling spices *(top right)*, as well as cider vinegar, enliven such favorites as Maine sweet pickles *(left)*, green tomato relish *(center)* and corn relish *(bottom right)*.

Lamb shoulder can become an elegant dish when filled with spinach stuffing and braced with fresh asparagus spears and new potatoes.

Braised Stuffed Shoulder of Lamb

In a heavy 12-inch skillet, melt 2 tablespoons of butter in 2 tablespoons of oil over moderate heat. When the foam begins to subside, add the chopped onions and chopped garlic and, stirring frequently, cook for about 5 minutes until they are soft but not brown. Add the spinach and green pepper and stir until most of the liquid in the pan has evaporated. With a rubber spatula, scrape the spinach mixture into a deep bowl.

Melt 6 tablespoons of the remaining butter in the same skillet. Add the bread crumbs and fry them over moderate heat, stirring frequently until they are a delicate golden color. Add the contents of the skillet to the spinach mixture, then stir in the finely chopped celery, nutmeg, 1 teaspoon of the salt and a few grindings of pepper. Taste for seasoning.

Lay the lamb flat, cut side up, on a work surface and sprinkle it with the remaining ½ teaspoon of salt and a few grindings of pepper. Spread the spinach stuffing mixture evenly over the lamb. Starting at one long side, carefully roll the lamb into a tight cylinder. Wrap one end of a 10-foot length of cord around the lamb about 1 inch from the end of the roll and knot it securely. Then, in spiral fashion, loop the cord around the length of the roll to within about 1 inch of the opposite end. Wrap the end of the spiral tightly around the lamb and knot it securely.

Preheat the oven to 325°. In a heavy casserole large enough to hold the lamb comfortably, melt the remaining 3 tablespoons of butter over moderate heat. When the foam begins to subside, add the sliced onion, carrot, coarsely chopped celery, and crushed garlic and, stirring frequently, cook for about 5 minutes until the vegetables are soft but not brown. Set the casserole aside off the heat.

Meanwhile, warm the remaining 3 tablespoons of oil in the reserved skillet until a light haze forms above it. Brown the rolled lamb in the hot oil, turning it frequently with tongs or a slotted spatula and regulating the heat so that it colors richly and evenly on all sides without burning. Transfer the lamb roll to the casserole. Then brown the lamb bones in the fat remaining in the skillet and add them to the casserole.

Pour off the fat from the skillet and in its place add the water. Bring to a boil over high heat, stirring constantly and scraping in the brown particles that cling to the bottom and sides of the pan. Pour the mixture over the lamb and drop in the tied parsley and bay leaf.

Cover the casserole tightly and braise the lamb in the middle of the oven for 1½ hours, or until it is tender and shows no resistance when pierced deeply with the point of a skewer or small, sharp knife.

Transfer the lamb to a heated platter and drape foil over it to keep it warm while you prepare the sauce. With tongs, remove the bones from the casserole and discard them. Then strain the liquid remaining in the casserole through a fine sieve into a small saucepan, pressing down hard on the vegetables and herbs with the back of a spoon to extract all their juices before discarding them.

Skim as much fat as possible from the surface of the stock and bring to a simmer over moderate heat. Stirring the stock constantly, pour in the arrowroot mixture and cook until the sauce comes to a boil, thickens lightly and is smooth. Remove from the heat, add the mustard and taste for seasoning. Pour the sauce into a bowl and serve at once with the lamb.

11 tablespoons butter

5 tablespoons vegetable oil

1 cup finely chopped onions plus, 1 small onion, peeled and sliced into ⅛-inch-thick rounds

1½ teaspoons finely chopped garlic plus 1 garlic clove, peeled and crushed with the side of a cleaver or heavy knife

1 pound fresh spinach, cooked, drained, squeezed completely dry and finely chopped, or substitute 2 cups thoroughly defrosted frozen chopped spinach, squeezed completely dry and finely chopped

½ cup finely chopped green bell pepper

3 cups soft fresh crumbs made from homemade-type white bread, pulverized in a blender or finely shredded with a fork

¼ cup finely chopped celery, plus 1 small celery stalk, coarsely chopped

¼ teaspoon ground nutmeg, preferably freshly grated

1½ teaspoons salt

Freshly ground black pepper

A 6- to 7-pound lamb shoulder, boned and flattened, with the bones sawed into small pieces and reserved

1 medium-sized carrot, scraped and cut into ⅛-inch-thick slices

2 cups water

4 sprigs fresh parsley and 1 medium-sized bay leaf tied with kitchen string

2 teaspoons arrowroot dissolved in ¼ cup cold water

1 tablespoon prepared mustard

VII

The Maple Sugar Mountains

In the melting snow of late winter, on a farm in the maple sugar country of northern Vermont, Mrs. Barbara Carpenter and her daughters care for an orphaned lamb. Mary, 11, gives the lamb its bottle while sister Susie, 8, and the dog Tippy stand by.

Five of the six New England states and all four of Canada's Maritime Provinces face the sea, and even in earliest times their settlers benefited from it. They had plenty of fish and seafood for their own use and for export too, and the ships they built out of the timber that grew close behind the shore put them in touch with each other and countries overseas. The coastal settlements and those on navigable rivers were never cut off from the world. People came and went bringing up-to-date ideas. The same vessels that carried salt fish, grain and lumber across the Atlantic returned with foodstuffs as well as manufactured goods.

This easy intercourse with the world had its effect on New England's cuisine. The characteristic dishes developed out of native products—corn, beans, seafood—remained popular, but foreign products quickly came into use. Perhaps the most important was molasses from the West Indies, which figured in many a New England recipe. Wines, brandy and raisins from the Mediterranean made an early appearance. New England seamen ranged farther, bringing tapioca from South America, dates from the Middle East, spices from Indonesia and tea and ginger from China. Many exotic ingredients were built into the cooking of New England when less venturesome places knew and used few if any of them.

One part of New England was different. Vermont and northern New Hampshire remained a wild frontier long after the rest of New England was well settled. Not only were they cold, mountainous and hard of access; they were dangerous country. The French had forts on Lake Champlain and claimed most of the territory between Quebec and the English settlements on the coast. For more than a century they and their Indian allies raided deep into New England. It took a brave, even reckless man to live in this borderland or to hunt in its woods. Few did. As late as 1760 only 300 people lived in the present state of Vermont.

The fall of New France in 1759 took the pressure off. The Indians, no longer encouraged and armed by the French, soon quieted down, and a wave of settlers moved into the mountains. At first they followed the major rivers—most of which had strips of fertile soil in their valley bottoms—and occupied the flatlands bordering Lake Champlain. These were hardy men who left their families behind and spent summer and autumn clearing a patch of land and building a rudimentary shelter. In the spring they returned with their families, a team of oxen and their meager household goods and planted enough food crops to keep them and their animals alive, with luck, through the winter. Not all of them made it; some died of cold, hunger and disease or retreated back to the safer settlements.

Most of the mountain settlers thrived in a rugged, homespun way. Their first cash crop was potash, made by leaching the ashes of the great hardwood trees they burned to clear land. Then came cattle. For a while Vermont was cattle country, with Green Mountain cowboys (on foot and often barefoot) driving the herds to market in Boston. When the cattle were sold, the drovers might buy a backpack of manufactured goods (cobblers' nails, ax heads and gunpowder, needles and thread) to carry back to the mountains.

Vermonters are independent still, but they were even more so in those frontier years. Before the American Revolution, Vermont was claimed by the colonial governments of both New York and New Hampshire, but after those colonies revolted and became states of the Union, its few inhabitants defied both claimants. For 14 years Vermont was a separate, if shaky republic. It coined money, set up post offices and naturalized the citizens of "foreign countries" such as Massachusetts. At last, in 1791, it made a satisfactory deal with the United States, ratified the Constitution and became the 14th state of the Union. Vermonters do not boast about their early nationhood as much as Texans do, but they are mindful of it in a quiet way, as modern visitors to the state find.

The population of Vermont increased from 85,425 in 1790 to 217,895 in 1810, and that of New Hampshire from 141,885 to 214,460. After fertile land grew scarce, the settlers pushed into the highlands, up the narrow twisting valleys whose level bottomlands were only a few yards wide, and where frost lingered late in June and returned in September. On these upland farms survival was an annual miracle, so after the War of 1812 when good land in the Northwest Territories (now the Middle West) was opened, some Vermonters left their state. Today hikers and hunters in the unbroken forest on the upper slopes of the Green Mountains sometimes come across the cellar holes and stone walls of the highwater mark of settlement.

Most Vermonters chose to stay instead of taking available land in easier climates. Stubbornly they clung to their villages, which are now among the loveliest places in the United States. They developed small industries such as making high quality tools and machines. They turned to dairy farming and cheese making. They even invented a kind of architecture all their own, with recessed porches set into the houses on the first and sometimes the second floor. Such porches get less snow, and their sheltered position makes them comfortable on days when ordinary porches would be too chilly. Few Vermonters grew rich, but nearly all did well enough by hard work to win self-respect. They preserved and improved a kind of life that harried city people cannot help but admire.

Modern Vermont is prosperous and still beautiful. Good roads lead to every hamlet, and strict laws keep them clear of billboards. The two-season tourist industry—vacationers in summer, skiers in winter—brings an increasing flow of money into the state. The main worry is about the future. The selectmen of the little towns watch with apprehension the ever-growing traffic on the new, fast highways that have brought three great and spreading cities—Boston, New York and Montreal—within easy driving distance. The selectmen shake their heads: "Each year they come closer and closer." With all due prudence they are planning defenses, but the state does not have the heart to keep its recipes that secret. Vermont cooking is essentially New England cooking minus most seafood and plus maple sugar and abundant cream. In the early years Atlantic salmon swarmed in the Connecticut River and landlocked salmon in Lake Champlain. They were so plentiful they were salted like codfish, and were considered such humble food that a regulation forbade feeding them to indentured servants more than once a week. That time of plenty passed quickly. Lake Champlain has few fish in it now, and any salmon trying to navigate the lower Connecticut River, which drains the sewage of city after city, would have to make the trip in a space suit. About the only fish that now plays a part in traditional Vermont cooking is salt codfish, which could always be brought from the seacoast by slow wagon transport without spoiling. It is cooked by the same recipe used in coastal New England except that the sauce served with it is apt to be made with lots of cream.

In place of seafood Vermont had beef and pork. One gets the impression that the beef was not tender. Oldtime recipes make little mention of steak and roasts; most beef was stewed, pot-roasted or chopped. Winter was the time for fresh beef: the animals were slaughtered in the fall when pasturage failed. By that time the weather was cool enough to keep the meat fresh until it froze hard. During cold spells it could be hung even in the kitchen without thawing. (The only tolerably warm place in the house was right in front of the fire.)

After the weather warmed up in the spring Vermonters depended on corned beef and salted and smoked pork products. Farmers and many non-farmers too made their own corned beef, selecting certain cuts and submerging them in large stone crocks of brine made with salt, sugar and a little saltpeter. Corned beef, incidentally, has nothing to do with corn. The name comes from the fact that saltpeter was handy in the form of gunpowder, which came in "corns" (grains). Homemade corned beef was never pink, but was grayish brown.

The best-known corned beef dish of New England, besides the ubiquitous corned beef and cabbage, is boiled dinner *(Recipe Index)*, the same standby dish that was often built around codfish in coastal areas.

Some Vermont cooks advocate boiling salt pork, the kind with lean strips in it, along with the beef. Vegetables are often added to the pot from time to time according to how long each takes to cook, but they may be cooked separately. Some authorities insist on parsnips as well as carrots, potatoes, cabbage and turnips. Others deplore parsnips. Beets are usually cooked by themselves so they will not color everything pink. When the meat and vegetables are all properly tender they are taken out and arranged tastefully on a large platter. The meat may be put in the center with the vegetables displayed in colorful rings around it, but it and the vegetables also may be piled in small mounds. The broth may be served as soup, and it is delicious.

There is a mystique about New England boiled dinner. Part of it is the compliment it pays to the men of the family. Just to look at it, marshaled magnificently on its platter, makes them feel big, strong, brave and able to cope with all adversities. Another part is the knowledge of what the leftovers will be made into. Good housewives always cook more boiled dinner than their families can eat. The remains are chopped (not ground) and pan-fried as red-flannel hash *(Recipe Index)*, originally a vegetable hash topped with meat slices. The redness, of course, comes from the beets, but both the color and the taste vary considerably according to the proportions of the ingredients. Some cooks moisten the hash, after it has started browning on the bottom, with a little boiled-dinner broth and serve it with a sprinkling of salt port or suet cracklings. Even without these touches, red-flannel hash is startling to the eye and excellent to the taste. Sometimes pork fried in this way is served with boiled vegetables as "salt pork dinner."

For insatiably hungry men who required massive fueling, salt pork was sometimes roasted. A thick chunk was soaked overnight in milk; then the rind was scored an inch deep and the gashes stuffed with seasoned bread crumbs. It was placed rind-down in a dish and baked with potatoes and a little milk until both potatoes and pork were pleasantly brown. Not many modern city men are man enough for it.

A proper companion for this powerful dish is old-fashioned Vermont fried pie. This is a super-rich pastry turnover filled with a sweet, cinnamon-flavored applesauce and deep-fried until brown *(Recipe Index)*. Smoked ham was cooked in the usual ways, boiled and then sometimes baked, but it was also chopped or ground and made into a goodly number of fine dishes, including soufflés and pies. Ham turnovers are ground ham and chopped onions in white sauce, enclosed in biscuit dough and baked. Ham shortcakes are buttermilk biscuits mixed with ground ham before baking and served with egg sauce. Stuffed ham roll is a slice of uncooked ham spread with buttered, seasoned crumbs, rolled and tied. It is put in a covered baking dish with a little water and baked until tender. Try it if you favor ham; you will favor it even more afterward.

The most distinctive element of New England mountain cooking was and is maple sugar. In the early years this was not considered a luxury; it was the ordinary sweetening agent that almost every settler made on his own place. Cane sugar or even molasses brought up from the coast by pack horse or sledge cost far more. The mountain people used maple sugar for all the purposes that other sweeteners serve. They also appreciated its de-

Opposite: In the mountain states of New England, familiar regional fare often gets an unusual twist. The Vermont chicken pie is covered with an array of baking-powder biscuits, and is served with maple-sweetened, creamed winter squash as well as cranberry sauce.

lightful flavor and developed many various ways to make the most of it.

The source of these delights is the sugar maple, a stately, gray-barked tree as beautiful as it is useful. It likes the cold and prefers places with bitter winters, and it does not mind growing on slopes too steep and rocky to serve as farmland or pasture. For farmers it has the important advantage of providing its crop—its sweet sap—at the very start of spring before their annual rush of plowing and planting begins.

No one seems to know for sure whether the Indians were the first to tap sugar maples. Some authorities think they hacked gashes in the bark with their tomahawks and arranged in some way, perhaps by an upward cut in the bark, to make the sap running down the gash drip away from the tree trunk and collect in a container. The first white settlers did it in this way, and perhaps the Indians did it before them, but it is not likely that the Indians boiled much of the sap to sugar or heavy syrup as some accounts have them doing. Before they got steel axes and saws from the Europeans they were not equipped to cut the great quantities of firewood needed to boil the sap, and they lacked effective vessels to boil it in. They are sometimes said to have put the sap in large wooden troughs and to have boiled it down by dropping hot stones in it. This would be inefficient, to put it mildly, and the syrup produced would be full of ashes, soot and burnt sugar. My own guess is that the Indians may have tapped the "sweetest" trees (they vary) and concentrated the sap a little by boiling it in the iron kettles that they bought from European traders long before Vermont was settled. At any rate this was the method the first settlers used. They had steel axes to gash the trees and cut firewood, and they also had large iron kettles for making their important cash crop, potash. They got double use out of the kettles by boiling maple sap.

This primitive method was soon superseded by one that is still used. Early in spring, weeks before the buds of the maples begin to swell, the farmer flounders through deep snow and drills ⅜- or ⁷⁄₁₆-inch holes 2½ inches into the sapwood. He hammers into each hole a galvanized iron spout and hangs on it a bucket that is covered so that sap drips into it but rain stays out. A tree 10 inches in diameter gets one bucket. Bigger trees get as many as five. Then the farmer waits for the first warmish day.

No one really knows what makes sap run except that it is part of the tree's preparation for the growing season. A sunny day or a warm wind is enough to start the clear, colorless sap dripping out of the spouts and plinking into the buckets. The flow usually but not always stops at night. Sometimes a cold wind blowing through the treetops is enough to stop it. The sap does not rise; most of it comes from above the tap hole, and a tree growing in the open with a spreading crown gives more than a crowded one. The sugar in the sap is a mystery too. One theory holds that it is formed by the tree as antifreeze to protect the living cells from frost.

During a heavy run the sap fills the buckets in a day, so the farmer is kept busy tending all the 1,000 trees of a typical sugarbush. He makes his rounds with a tractor or a team of horses pulling a tank on a sledge, and brings the sap back to the sugarhouse where it will be boiled down to syrup. An easier but less picturesque method that is coming into use is to attach thin plastic tubes to the spouts. The sap from dozens of trees runs

Opposite: The Homestead Inn's version of New England boiled dinner is different in including dried horticultural shell beans *(at bottom on the platter)* among its vegetables, along with sliced rutabaga, beets, potatoes, carrots and quarters of cabbage.

downhill to tanks, or to pipelines leading to the sugarhouse. The sap flows for several weeks in fits and starts. One of the things that can stop the run is the healing of the wood tissues around the tap hole.

A good many years ago an unusually bright farmer reasoned that since sanitation is generally a good thing, it might apply to tapping trees. So he carefully sterilized his drills and spouts and was delighted to find that his trees gave sap much longer than his neighbor's did. He kept his mouth shut, of course, and his neighbor did not inquire. That would have been un-Vermont behavior. But he noticed the longer run of sap, and after a number of years he leaned on the fence between the two sugarbushes one day. "I sort of wonder," he remarked delicately, "why this little fence makes so much difference."

There is a good deal of mystery about the delightful flavor of maple syrup. The flavor is not in the sap as it drips from the tree. If the sap is boiled down in a vacuum pan at low temperature, the resulting syrup has hardly any taste except sweetness. Apparently when the sap is boiled, in a kettle, tasteless minor constituents turn into maple flavor. But the boiling (it takes about 30½ gallons—a legal barrel—of sap to make one gallon of syrup) must be done just right. If not, the syrup gets darker and thicker with a stronger flavor that is less popular today. The settlers' syrup, boiled slowly with butter to enrich it, was probably very dark indeed.

Old recipes from the mountains of New England use maple sugar or syrup in almost anything. The settlers even brewed a sort of beer by fermenting weak syrup. They favored maple sugar instead of molasses in baked beans *(Recipe Index)* and mincemeat. They simmered hams and sausages with maple syrup. What they were doing, of course, was using home-produced maple products as cheap and handy substitutes for store-bought sweeteners. The taste of the final product was not very different.

Such archaic recipes are a waste nowadays, or at least an extravagant use of good (and expensive) maple syrup. The delightful maple flavor is subtle and delicate; it is overwhelmed by powerful flavors such as those of smoked ham. Much more successful are recipes that use maple sugar by itself or combined with only mild ingredients. There is no lack of these. Maple sugar or syrup is great in frostings, ice cream, candies and sauces for pouring on ice cream or puddings. Here it has little or no competition from rival sweeteners and can be appreciated to the fullest.

A favorite Vermont dessert is maple sugar pie, which can be made with one crust or two, or can be covered with meringue. The filling calls for milk or cream (that other Vermont favorite) and is stiffened with eggs and flour. Sometimes nutmeg is sprinkled on top; if used sparingly it does not damage the maple flavor. Maple chiffon pie, made like other kinds of chiffon pie with maple syrup substituted for sugar, is also excellent. The old recipes often call for chopped butternuts, but these are hard to get if you do not have butternut trees and plenty of industrious children. Unsalted pecans are just as good.

Maple combines very well with apples. For maple-baked apples just pare and core your apples and put into each one before baking a couple of tablespoons of soft maple sugar. This delicious ingredient comes in cans or jars and has about the consistency of peanut butter. Like all maple

 Continued on page 163

Covers protect the sap from dirt. Each taphole *(below)* may produce, drop by drop, 12 quarts of sap on a good day.

A 20-Million-Gallon Crop, Harvested Drop by Drop

Cold and clear as spring water, the sap of Vermont's stately sugar maple trees begins to run at the first stirrings of warm weather, and flows for a few brief weeks in March and early April. In that time, the state's 14,000 sugar makers, whose techniques have barely changed in 150 years, gather up to 20 million gallons of sap. They struggle up snow-covered hillsides to collect each day's run by hand and often toil far into the night in the sugarhouse, boiling off the sap into syrup. The work is grueling, but when the first pitcher of rich, new syrup arrives at the dining table, along with a batch of fresh doughnuts, it vindicates the sugar maker's age-old claim: "By Gory, after all is said and done, sugaring is fun!"

During the hectic weeks of sap collecting, everyone in the family lends a hand. Here Charles Carpenter pours a pailful of sap into his horse-drawn gathering tank. His wife Barbara *(background)*, their elder daughter Mary, and Charles Pilbin, a farm hand *(left)*, help collect the day's run from other trees. The Carpenter sugarbush has 1,400 trees and produces 200 to 300 gallons of syrup a season.

In late afternoon on the Carpenter farm, Charles Pilbin drives the gathering rig to the sugarhouse to boil off the day's yield of maple sap.

Barbara Carpenter pours newly made maple syrup through a felt filter to remove all traces of sediment before canning.

By carefully controlled reheating, the syrup can be transformed into various other maple products such as maple cream *(left, above)*, which is delicious on hot toast or as cake icing, maple candies *(top)*, or granulated maple sugar, at bottom in antique glass scoop. Soft maple sugar, at left of the maple syrup, is used in baking apple pie or beans. Old-fashioned grained sugar *(right)*, which has a more granular texture than the candies, is sold in blocks from which sugar is shaved off or grated for use in cooking.

Vermont maple syrup is strictly graded according to color—one key to its quality. From left, Fancy Grade, the finest, is a light amber with a delicate flavor. Grade A is slightly darker, with a stronger flavor. Grade B, still darker, with a caramel taste, is generally used for cooking. "Unclassified," the fourth grade is darkest, and is used in commercial maple and blended syrups.

products it is expensive, and it should be kept locked up or someone in the family will devour it all in a day or two.

Any fruit or vegetable whose own flavor is not too strong is raised to new heights by a judicious lacing with maple. This applies to peaches and pears, sweet potatoes and baked acorn squash *(Recipe Index)*. My wife, who is Peruvian, uses maple syrup with excellent results in a typical Latin-American dish, baked bananas. She slices peeled ripe bananas lengthwise and packs them as closely as possible in a baking pan, flat side up. She dribbles a few drops of lemon juice on each and arranges symmetrically two or three pea-size bits of butter. Then, instead of the brown sugar usually used, she pours a teaspoon or so of maple syrup over each slice. She bakes them in a moderate oven until they are soft and puts them under the broiler for a few minutes before serving. Baked bananas with brown sugar are good; with maple they are better.

Apple pies get a boost from maple syrup and so do squash and pumpkin pies if their spices are not so strong that they mask the maple flavor. Almost any unspiced or lightly spiced cake is improved if maple syrup is substituted for cane sugar, and many kinds of cookies that call for molasses can be made with maple syrup instead and be the better for it.

In general the simplest maple recipes are the best. A little maple syrup added to milk makes it a glorious drink that beguiles the most obstinate milk-resistant children. Soft maple sugar makes cakelike sandwiches that few can pass up. Toast, buttered and sprinkled with granulated maple sugar and put in the broiler for a minute or so, is like no other toast. Alternatively, use block maple sugar and grate it with a cheese grater.

The simplest and most famous of all maple recipes calls for nothing but syrup and snow. In places that make maple sugar, the "sugaring off party" is an old and beloved tradition. Toward the end of the tapping season when the rush of work is over, the man who operates a sugarbush invites his friends, and especially their children, to the sugarhouse where his syrup is boiling. The guests are given dishes of clean snow brought from the dense evergreen woods where snowbanks linger in the shade, and as they file past, the host pours hot syrup onto the snow. Instantly the syrup hardens to the world's most wonderful candy, waxlike, ice-cold, powerfully sweet. You can eat more if you alternate with (believe it or not) sour pickles, which are usually supplied. The trick with the syrup is to boil it until a candy thermometer reads 230°. Or 232° if you like the snow candy harder.

When I was a boy I went to an informal sugaring off that I still remember vividly. My great-aunt Eliza owned a sugarbush near Greenfield, Massachusetts. It was rented to a farmer whose son met my father and me at a railroad station with a Model T Ford and took us up a narrow valley to the sugarhouse among the groves of maples. Other people were invited too. I remember much laughing and screaming from the kids. There was no snow in sight, but presently the farmer went to a great pile of evergreen boughs. He pulled some away. Underneath was a heap of snow as clean as when it fell from the sky. Then he went into the sugarhouse and reappeared with a tin dipper of hot syrup. I could hardly wait while he poured it in amber spirals on the snow. We all grabbed. I can taste it still.

Opposite: At the end of the short maple season, Susie Carpenter, at left, throws a traditional "Sugar-in-Snow" party for two boys from a nearby farm. On a snow mound outside the sugarhouse, cooked maple syrup is poured over bowls of clean snow, where it hardens into a taffylike consistency. Raised doughnuts and sour pickles complete the children's feast.

Maple Bread Pudding

Brush a 4-cup steamed-pudding mold (or substitute any other 4-cup mold or pudding basin) with 1 teaspoon of softened butter.

If the maple sugar is moist, grate it on the finest side of a stand-up hand grater. If it is dry, grate it with a nut grinder. (There should be about ¾ cup of maple sugar.) Place the grated sugar in the pudding mold and, with your fingers, press it firmly against the bottom and sides to create a ⅛-inch-thick sugar shell inside the mold.

Spread each bread slice with ½ teaspoon of the remaining softened butter, then cut the slices into ½-inch cubes and gently drop them into the sugar-lined mold. In a deep bowl, beat the eggs with a wire whisk or a rotary or electric beater until they are frothy. Beat in the cream, milk and vanilla. Pour the mixture over the bread cubes and set the lid of the mold in place. (If the mold does not have a lid, cover it tightly with a double thickness of heavy-duty aluminum foil and tie the foil securely in place with kitchen string.) Place the mold on a rack set in a large pot, pour in enough boiling water to come halfway up the sides of the mold, and cover the pot tightly. Return the water to a boil over high heat, then reduce the heat to the lowest possible setting and simmer for 1½ hours. Lift the mold from the pot and remove the lid or foil.

The pudding can be served hot or cold, with or without unsweetened whipped cream, but should be unmolded only just before serving. To unmold it, run a thin-bladed knife around the sides of the mold and place a shallow serving bowl upside down over the top. Grasping the bowl and mold together firmly, invert them. The pudding should slide out easily.

To serve 6

3 teaspoons butter, softened
6 ounces maple sugar
4 slices homemade-type white bread, each cut about ½ inch thick, with all crusts removed
4 eggs
1 cup light cream
1 cup milk
2 teaspoons vanilla extract

Maple-Walnut Fudge Balls

With a pastry brush, spread the softened butter evenly over the bottom and sides of an 8-by-6-by-2-inch baking dish.

If the maple sugar is moist, grate it on the finest side of a stand-up hand grater. If it is dry, grate it with a nut grinder. (There should be about 2 cups, packed, of grated maple sugar.) Combine the maple sugar, white sugar, cream and cream of tartar in a heavy 3- to 4-quart saucepan. Bring to a boil over high heat, stirring until the sugar dissolves. Reduce the heat and boil slowly, uncovered and undisturbed, until the syrup reaches a temperature of 240° on a candy thermometer, or until a few drops spooned into ice water immediately form a soft ball.

Pour the fudge into the buttered dish, cool to room temperature, then chill in the refrigerator for at least 3 hours. Transfer the fudge to a deep bowl and, with an electric beater or wooden spoon, beat it until light and creamy. Pinch off about 1 tablespoon of the fudge and roll it between the palms of your hands until it forms a ball about 1 inch in diameter. Roll it gently in the pulverized walnuts and when the entire surface is lightly coated set it aside on a platter. Refrigerate until ready to serve.

To make about 36 one-inch balls

1 teaspoon butter, softened
1 pound maple sugar
1 cup sugar
1 cup heavy cream
½ teaspoon cream of tartar
1 cup walnuts, pulverized in a blender or with a nut grinder

Vermont maple sugar or syrup lends flavor and scent to three sweets. From left, steamed maple bread pudding (to serve hot or cold), maple-walnut fudge balls, maple-custard pie with rum cream and walnuts.

To make about 2 quarts

1¼ pounds maple sugar
2 cups milk
2 eggs
⅓ cup flour
3 cups heavy cream, chilled
1 cup coarsely chopped walnuts,
    optional

Maple Sugar Ice Cream

If the maple sugar is moist, use the finest side of a stand-up hand grater to grate enough to make 1 cup firmly packed, and chop the rest of the maple sugar into ¼-inch bits with a large, sharp knife. If the maple sugar is dry, grate it with a nut grinder to make 1 cup.

Place the remaining ungrated maple sugar between pieces of wax paper and break it into small bits with the smooth surface of a kitchen mallet or with the side of a heavy cleaver. (There should be about 1½ cups of the maple sugar bits.)

In a heavy 3- to 4-quart saucepan, warm the milk over moderate heat until small bubbles appear around the edges of the pan. Cover to keep the milk warm and set aside off the heat.

Beat the eggs and the 1 cup of grated maple sugar together with a wire whisk or a rotary or electric beater. When the mixture begins to cling to the beater, sprinkle the flour over it. Continue to beat until the mixture falls in a slowly dissolving ribbon when the beater is lifted.

Beating constantly, pour in the hot milk in a thin stream. Return the mixture to the saucepan and stir over low heat until it becomes a custard thick enough to lightly coat the back of a metal spoon. (Do not let the custard come to a boil or it may curdle.) Remove the pan from the heat and let the custard cool to room temperature.

In a chilled bowl, whip the cream with a whisk or a rotary or electric beater until it is stiff enough to stand in soft peaks on the beater. With a rubber spatula, fold the cream gently but thoroughly into the cool custard. When no traces of white show, fold in the 1½ cups of maple sugar bits and the walnuts, if you are using them.

Pack a 2-quart ice cream freezer with layers of finely crushed or cracked ice and coarse rock salt in the proportions recommended by the freezer manufacturer. Add cold water if the manufacturer advises it. Then ladle the ice cream into the ice cream can and cover it.

If you have a hand ice cream maker, fill it with the ice cream and let it stand for 3 or 4 minutes before beginning to turn the handle. It may take 15 minutes or more of turning for the ice cream to freeze, but do not stop turning at any time or the ice cream may be lumpy.

When the handle can barely be moved, the ice cream is ready to serve. If you wish to keep it for an hour or two, remove the lid and dasher. Scrape the ice cream off the dasher and pack it firmly in the container with a spoon. Cover securely, pour off any water in the bucket and repack the ice and salt solidly around it. If you have an electric ice cream maker, fill and cover the can, turn it on and let it churn for about 15 minutes, or until the motor slows or actually stops. Serve the ice cream immediately or follow the procedure above to keep it for an hour or two.

Lacking an ice cream maker, pour the ice cream into 2 ice-cube trays from which the dividers have been removed, spreading it evenly and smoothing the top with the spatula. Freeze for 3 to 4 hours, stirring every 30 minutes or so and scraping into it the ice particles that form around the edges of the tray.

Tightly covered, the ice cream may safely be kept in the freezer for several weeks. Before serving, place it in the refrigerator for 20 or 30 minutes to let it soften slightly so that it can easily be served.

Vermont Chicken Pie

Remove the chunks of fat from the cavity of the chicken, cut them into small bits and reserve them. Truss the bird securely and place it in a heavy 7- to 8-quart (preferably oval-shaped) casserole. Scatter the onions, celery, parsley and bay leaf, thyme, 1 teaspoon of salt and a few grindings of pepper around the chicken and pour in 1 quart of water.

Bring to a boil over high heat, reduce the heat to low and place the lid on the casserole. Poach the chicken for about 1 hour and 15 minutes. To test for doneness, pierce the thigh of the bird with the point of a small, sharp knife. The juice that trickles out should be a clear yellow; if it is slightly pink, poach the bird for another 5 to 10 minutes.

Transfer the chicken to a platter and strain the cooking stock through a fine sieve into a bowl, pressing down hard on the vegetables and herbs with the back of a spoon to extract all their juices before discarding them. Measure and reserve 2½ cups of the stock. When the chicken is cool enough to handle, remove the skin and pull the meat from the bones with your fingers or a small knife. Discard the skin and bones and cut the meat into 1-inch pieces.

Drop the reserved bits of chicken fat into a heavy 10- to 12-inch skillet, add 2 tablespoons of water and cook over moderate heat, stirring frequently. When the bits have rendered all their fat, remove them from the skillet with a slotted spoon and discard them.

Add 2 tablespoons of butter to the chicken fat and melt over moderate heat. When the foam begins to subside, stir in 6 tablespoons of flour and mix to a smooth paste. Pour in the 2½ cups of reserved chicken stock and, stirring constantly with a wire whisk, cook over high heat until the sauce comes to a boil, thickens heavily and is smooth. Reduce the heat to low and simmer uncovered for about 5 minutes.

Stir in ½ teaspoon of salt and the white pepper and taste for seasoning. Remove the skillet from the heat, add the chicken pieces and toss together gently but thoroughly. Pour the entire contents of the pan into a 7-by-7-by-2-inch baking-serving dish and spread the pieces of chicken evenly over the bottom of the dish.

To prepare the biscuits, preheat the oven to 450°. Combine 2 cups of flour, the baking powder and 1 teaspoon of salt and sift them into a large chilled bowl. Add the butter bits and lard and, with your fingertips, rub the flour and fat together until they look like flakes of coarse meal. Pour in the milk and beat with a wooden spoon until the dough is smooth and can be gathered into a fairly dry, compact ball. If the dough remains moist and sticky, beat in up to ¼ cup more flour by the tablespoonful.

Place the dough on a lightly floured surface and roll it out into a rough rectangle about ⅓ inch thick. With a cookie cutter or the rim of a glass, cut the dough into 2-inch round biscuits. Gather the scraps together, roll them out again and cut out as many more rounds as you can. Ideally you should have about 12 biscuits.

Place the biscuits side by side over the chicken in the baking dish, arranging them so that they cover the top completely. Brush the biscuits with the melted butter and bake in the middle of the oven for about 25 minutes, or until the biscuits have puffed and are golden brown. Serve at once, directly from the baking dish.

A 4½- to 5-pound roasting chicken
3 large onions, peeled and cut crosswise into ¼-inch-thick slices
1 cup coarsely chopped celery, including the green leaves
4 sprigs fresh parsley and 1 small bay leaf tied together with kitchen string
¼ teaspoon crumbled dried thyme
1½ teaspoons salt
Freshly ground black pepper
1 quart plus 2 tablespoons water
2 tablespoons butter
6 tablespoons flour
½ teaspoon ground white pepper

BISCUITS
2 to 2¼ cups all-purpose flour
1 tablespoon double-acting baking powder
1 teaspoon salt
2 tablespoons butter, chilled and cut into ¼-inch bits plus ¼ cup butter, melted
2 tablespoons lard, chilled and cut into ¼-inch bits
½ cup cold milk

VIII

North of the Border: a French Flavor

At dusk on New Year's day, Laurent Valade lights the candles at a cheerfully decorated window in his home outside Montreal —to the delight of some young guests invited to share in the holiday's traditional ceremonies, which have included an ample afternoon meal.

When you drive north from Boston and get beyond its cluttered industrial complex, you pass through forested mountains and serene villages that are much like the New England of a century ago. The lanky, laconic inhabitants look like storybook Yankees but long before you approach the Canadian border you begin to encounter—in Maine, New Hampshire and Vermont—a different, un–New England people. They are somewhat shorter, darker of skin and hair and more vivacious seeming. If you ask directions of one of them, particularly an older person, likely as not you may get a reply in French.

These are French Canadians whose forebears moved into northern New England from the province of Quebec several generations ago. They live in tight communities centered around Catholic churches and tenaciously hold to the language of their homeland. You will see French-Canadian restaurants, but if you could eat in French-Canadian homes you would find a different cuisine, a blend of French, New England and native Canadian, the product of an old, isolated but still vigorous culture. The fount of this culture—and its cooking—is Canada's province of Quebec, *La Belle Province* as its citizens proudly call it.

Long before the English colonized New England, France marked the Gulf of Saint Lawrence and the great river behind it as a road to empire. As early as 1500, perhaps even earlier, French fishermen regularly crossed the Atlantic in small ships to exploit the rich fisheries around Newfoundland. Gradually they penetrated neighboring waters and the news drifted back to France that behind the forbidding outer islands was a pleasant

169

land open to any taker. In 1534 and 1535, Jacques Cartier, an explorer employed by King Francis I of France, felt out the region, claimed it formally and named it Canada after the Indian word *kanata,* which means town. He sailed up the Saint Lawrence, hoping that the river would lead to China, but was stopped by the foaming rapids above the present site of Montreal. In 1541 he returned with an ambitious colonizing expedition including 300 soldiers, many skilled artisans and even a few women. The settlement Cartier founded on the river lasted only two seasons; the tough climate proved too much for the inexperienced colonists, who mutinied and forced a return to France.

This setback ended official French interest in Canada for 60 years, but French fishermen made the dangerous voyage in ever greater numbers. They arrived in spring, planted small gardens on sheltered harbors and set up wooden platforms to dry their catch. Toward the end of summer larger vessels from the mother country picked up the dried fish and took them to market in France and around the Mediterranean. This informal traffic kept French interest in Canada alive until the end of the 16th Century, when a trend in men's fashions suddenly made the region important. In the late 1500s, as the fashion for trimming clothes with fur spread among the glittering noblemen of Europe, the price of pelts began to soar out of sight. Then came the discovery that the soft underfur of beavers could be made into fuzzy felt hats of incomparable quality. Every person of importance or would-be importance promptly demanded a beaver hat and would pay almost anything for it. All beavers were in jeopardy and the Saint Lawrence Basin, with its innumerable lakes and streams, was teeming with them. French fishermen stopped their fishing to trade with the Indians, often buying their beaver-skin cloaks off their backs. Adventurous Frenchmen took off into the forests as *coureurs de bois* (literally woods runners) to move from tribe to tribe collecting precious pelts.

When the French government realized the new commercial value of its long-neglected Canadian claims, it sent fresh expeditions to colonize them. Most were failures or only marginally successful, but in 1607 Samuel de Champlain founded a lasting settlement at Quebec. (The name in the local Indian language means "a closing together," where the Saint Lawrence River narrows to pass around a large island, the Ile d'Orléans.)

New France thus antedated New England by 13 years, but it did not have the quick and solid success of the English colonies. The Pilgrims and Puritans came as viable communities with women, children and a successful system of self-government. They did not look backward to England. As refugees from religious persecution they intended to make permanent homes as best they could in the New World. Few of the early French colonists had any such intention. They were almost all men; many were soldiers, and nearly all the rest were employees of government-sponsored monopolies who hoped to return to France after making quick fortunes in the fur trade.

But in Nova Scotia a first wave of French colonization already had taken firm root a year or so before the Quebec settlement. A small party of French peasants, including women, was brought by a colonizing company and set down at the mouth of the fertile Annapolis Valley on the

Bay of Fundy. With little hope of riches to distract them, they developed into a community of independent frontier farmers. This was Acadia, perhaps named after Arcadia in ancient Greece, perhaps after an Indian word meaning "fertile land." Neglected by the mother country and free of royal interference, the Acadians prospered in their forgotten corner of the world and earned the reputation of leading the idyllic life that Longfellow idealized in his poem *Evangeline:*

> *Every house was an inn, where all were welcomed and feasted;*
> *For with this simple people, who lived like brothers together,*
> *All things were held in common, and what one had was another's.*

The rest of New France had little peace or freedom. Wars with the Indians, especially the ferocious Iroquois of upper New York State, kept the settlements on the Saint Lawrence in constant peril. The population grew very slowly. Few Frenchmen emigrated to Canada under their own power, and many of those brought there by the king's agents preferred the wild, free life of *coureurs de bois* to working as peasants on the feudal estates granted to *seigneurs* by the French Crown.

The scarcity of women was such that the royal government took to importing shiploads of them, about 1,000 in all. Some of these *filles du roi,* or king's girls, came from orphanages, others from peasant families in northwestern France. They were given a dowry of provisions and household goods and were married off promptly. Those who accumulated 10 living children earned a royal pension and could try for an additional bonus by producing two more. Most present-day French Canadians are descended from the king's girls.

They must have been of sound stock, for they produced some exceedingly vigorous posterity. However, not all their contemporaries admired the way the girls were parceled out. A gossipy commentator of the time, Baron de La Hontan, wrote: "The Vestal Virgins were heaped up, (if I may so speak) one above another in three different apartments, where the bridegrooms singled out their Brides, just as a butcher does an Ewe from amongst a flock of sheep. . . . And indeed the market had such a run, that in fifteen days they were all disposed of. I am told the fattest went off best, upon the apprehension that those being less active would keep truer to their ingagements and hold out better against the nipping cold of the Winter."

Such measures raised the population of the Saint Lawrence colonies a little, but in 1673 it was only about 6,700, a pitifully small number to carry out the great plan that Louis XIV, the "Sun King," and his minister Colbert had conceived for French domination of North America. Daring explorers, mostly missionary priests, had shown that the Saint Lawrence offered the most direct route to the Great Lakes and the wonderfully fertile Mississippi Valley. If the French could occupy this rich hinterland they would confine the English colonists to the Atlantic seaboard and rule the better part of the continent.

The strategy was part of the long worldwide duel fought by England and France during the 17th and 18th Centuries. The North American phase called for population, which New France lacked. In a series of bloody wars, the French in Canada (who numbered at the most 60,000 compared to 1,500,000 people in the English colonies) fought amazingly well, sometimes supported by Indian allies and troops from France, sometimes on their own. But eventually they lost. Outlying garrisons were captured or driven back to the Saint Lawrence. Acadia was conquered and most of the 10,000 Acadians were expelled (as described in *Evangeline*) and distributed among the English colonies. The end came with the British capture of the city of Quebec in 1759. French soldiers and officials and many of the wealthier class sailed back to France.

Then came an amazing change. The French who stayed in Canada, now freed of war and royal regulation, began to thrive and multiply in their empty, fertile land much as the English colonists were doing in theirs. Hardly any additional immigrants came from France, which was soon cut off spiritually from intensely Catholic French Canada by the antireligious French Revolution of 1789. But left largely to their own devices by their British overlords, who valued them as a counterpoise to their own rebellious colonists, the French-speaking Canadians increased from about 60,000 at the Treaty of Paris in 1763 to just over a million in 1867 at the time of the Canadian Confederation. There are now around six and one half million of them.

Even the dispossessed Acadians made a comeback. Some emerged from hiding in the woods of Nova Scotia and New Brunswick. Others filtered back from places of exile as far away as the West Indies; some are said to have walked all the way from Louisiana. They cleared new farms in the forest or took to fishing or lumbering. Now they are found in many parts of the Maritime Provinces, where they keep up their own traditions while getting along amicably with their English-speaking neighbors.

The French-Canadian cuisine is not as distinctive as that of New England. That is, it is more like the food of France than New England food is like that of England. The reasons for this are historical. For one thing, the New Englanders were determined to be as independent of England as possible from the beginning and so were more in the mood to invent dishes and cooking techniques of their own. Then too, English cooking never had high prestige, not in the 17th Century or today, so as the New Englanders became more prosperous and sophisticated they did not feel it necessary to import English cooks to manage the kitchens of inns or wealthy houses. They adopted some English ideas, such as tea drinking, which came from the Far East via England, but they felt with justice that their own cooking was as good as that of England. Why imitate?

The French Canadians, at least those in Quebec, had a different attitude. While their country was part of France it was governed tightly from Paris, and its officials brought, or tried to bring, the latest French culture with them. In the 17th Century French cooking, except among the nobility, was not as elaborate as it is now, but later it acquired such enormous prestige that its influence was hard to resist. The wealthier and better-educated French-Canadian families did not resist, and they do not today. In modern Montreal, a very sophisticated city, most of the best restaurants try to keep as close as possible to French cooking. Many well-to-do private households do the same, and French-Canadian cookbooks

Continued on page 176

A Homecoming Feast to Start the New Year

For many French Canadian families the first day of the new year heralds the Catholic ceremony of *bénédiction,* in which the grandfather of the family asks God's blessing on them all for the coming year. Then everyone settles down to a winter feast of roast pork and—for the grownups—*caribou,* a homemade wine-and-spirit drink. In the picture above Laurent Valade, 18, returns to his home near Montreal from a new-year's ride, to help his parents prepare for the party. Soon others of the family arrive, including Laurent's married sister Francine and her two children. When the guest of honor, *grand-père* Eugène Valade, 84 *(right)* enters, festivities can start.

Left: The gathering begins solemnly, as Eugène Valade invokes God's blessing on three generations of his family—and Laurent's friend Michelle Nolet, at far left.

After the blessing, Francine's daughter Julie and a friend take a look at the Christmas crêche. *Right:* Granddaughter Julie watches Madame Paul Valade ladle gravy onto the garlic-flavored pork roast before carving it. Among the dishes surrounding the roast are marinated beets, at top, and *(reading clockwise)* fruit, homemade bread for the *cretons de Québec* (a pâté of pork, onions and leaf lard), a maple syrup pie garnished with chopped walnuts, *sucre à la crème* (a candy of light brown and white sugar and light cream), served with chocolates, and a decanter of *caribou*—a potent homemade mixture of spirits and red wine.

feature recipes that are called Canadian but are hard to distinguish from their equivalents in France.

In spite of long hostility between French Canada and New England, there was a lot of intermingling. After the American War of Independence, some of the "Empire Loyalists" who emigrated to Canada settled in Quebec and brought their cooking customs with them. Recipes given in French-Canadian books still include classic New England dishes that have become Canadianized, such as Boston baked beans *(fèves au lard du Québec)* and fish chowder *(chowder de poisson)*. Even steamed brown bread, that utterly New England item, is appreciated in the kitchens of French Canada as *pain brun*.

A true French-Canadian cuisine does exist nevertheless, and it has many dishes that French chefs never heard of and many more that have been sharply modified. Good use is made of native ingredients such as corn, blueberries and maple sugar that are little known in France. Garlic is less important than in most French cooking, and pork is the most popular meat. As is natural for outdoor people in a very cold country, pork fat is welcomed, not avoided.

Some French Canadians seem ashamed of their native cooking, perhaps because it was the product of a farming population, not of noble *châteaux* or elegant cosmopolites. This attitude is going out of fashion. In spite of continuing enthusiasm for the culture and cooking of France, there is growing interest in French Canada's own traditions. Attractive restaurants are beginning to appear that specialize in *recettes Canadiennes,* and in Montreal leading chefs are making a serious attempt to adapt traditional dishes to modern uses, which usually means reducing their complexity and fat content. With plenty of heat in their buildings and automobiles, modern Canadians are not forced to battle the cold so vigorously and therefore demand less fuel in their food.

True to its French background, French-Canadian cooking uses more herbs and spices than New England cooking does. The Acadians of Nova Scotia, for instance, put bay leaves in their fish chowders, giving them a subtly different flavor. Sometimes they also add celery, celery leaves, carrots and thyme. Fish steaks that are to be broiled may be basted with a butter sauce containing lemon juice, grated onion, pepper, salt and tarragon or thyme. When served they are often garnished with paprika and parsley. Meat may be cooked with a great variety of seasonings according to taste. Some of the recipes, like the traditional yule log *(bûche de Noël)* or the delicious pork *pâté* known as *cretons (Recipe Index),* take time and trouble, but French Canadians have inherited from their ancestors in France the admirable conviction that taking trouble about food is the best possible way to spend one's time.

The indispensable cooking utensil of rural French Canada was the black iron kettle that hung by a hook in the open fireplace. (To have a housewarming, always the occasion for a gay party, was to *prendre la crémaillère,* literally take the pothook.) Kettles were also essential in early New England, but even a loyal New Englander like myself has to admit that more thoughtful, painstaking cooking was done in Canadian kettles, which had behind them the long tradition of French kettle cookery.

Among the kettles' products were many kinds of soup. The standby fare of French Canada—so standby that it is joked about—is pea soup *(Recipe Index)*. Like most folk dishes it has many versions. The simplest is made of whole yellow peas soaked overnight, boiled until they are soft and flavored with celery leaves and with onions fried in pork fat. More elaborate versions are built around a ham bone or a considerable quantity of smoked pork boiled with the peas, which may be split, that is, skinless and quicker to cook. Diced potatoes and chopped celery are sometimes added and cooked just long enough to make them tender. The soup makes a complete meal and a good one.

Other nourishing soups are based on cabbage, carrots, potatoes or other vegetables. They usually start with beef bones to give them substance and are flavored with onions and herbs. A popular potato chowder contains not only milk, onions and potatoes but also carrots, celery, parsley, tarragon and grated cheese. In the old days soups like this were commonly served for breakfast. For even more massive meals the soup might have both beans and chopped beef.

Soups were only the beginning of kettle cookery. The cuisine of French Canada offers an almost unlimited number of stews and ragouts. Most of them seem familiar enough to non-French eyes, but they usually have a distinctive flavor derived from deft touches of herbs and spices, garlic and shallots. The most elaborate dish of this sort, which may also be called a pie, is *cipâte (Recipe Index)*. It has many other names *(cipaille, si-paille, six-pates,* sea-pie) in different French dialects and in the various English attempts to spell them.

In the early years *cipâte* was made of rabbit, venison or other game, but it can be made just as well with store-bought meat so long as enough kinds are used. A typical recipe calls for chicken, pork, veal and beef. Together with four or five kinds of vegetables they are stacked in layers in a heavy kettle or Dutch oven and covered with pie crust. Some authorities insist that the uncooked *cipâte* be put in the refrigerator overnight so the flavors can mingle. Next day chicken stock is poured through holes in the pie crust and the kettle is put in the oven, tightly covered, for three or four hours of baking. More stock is added from time to time to compensate for evaporation, and the cover is removed for 20 minutes at the end to brown the crust. The result is not only a magnificent stew (or pie) but a monument to French-Canadian housewifely devotion.

In the old days every *habitant* (farmer) who could do so kept pigs and made excellent use of their meat on the table. Almost every part was used. The head was made into headcheese. This is still done in many modern households, but often a more sightly cut such as the shoulder is substituted for the head. Any small scraps of meat, either fat or lean, become *gratons de Québec* (also known as *cretons de Québec),* a kind of meat pâté which is made by chopping the meat fine and simmering it slowly with lots of lard, onions and many seasonings *(Recipe Index).* After grinding, it is poured into a bowl or soup plate, where it solidifies enough to be eaten as a canapé or spread on bread.

When the French Canadians bake a roast of pork, say a loin, they do not merely put it in the oven. They pin onion rings on it with toothpicks

178

and during the last half-hour of baking they baste it lovingly with a glaze of brown sugar, cornstarch and vinegar, which forms a glorious crust and helps the onion rings flavor the fat underneath. With some pork roasts they serve gravy made by browning a little flour in the fat left in the roasting pan, but another way of using the fat is more traditional. After the roast is taken out, some of the fat is poured off. A cup of water is added to the pan and stirred around to dissolve the brown bits on the bottom. Then both fat and water are poured into a bowl and chilled. The fat hardens into what is essentially lard. The watery part turns into a dark brown, bouncy jelly with an intense meaty flavor. The two of them together comprise *graisse de rôti,* or drippings; it is used as a spread on bread and is much better than it sounds. Actually it contains less fat than butter does.

A characteristic French-Canadian dish is the meat pie. There seems to be a deep-rooted habit of putting a pastry crust on almost anything and popping it in the oven. Not a bad habit either; the crust augments the dish, captures flavors trying to escape and adds a bit of drama when the dish is served. In some cases it acts as a wrapping that makes the contents easier to handle and store.

Certain pies are traditionally served on religious holidays. The special pie for Easter has sliced hard-boiled eggs laid down on the bottom crust. Next come thin slices of cooked pork, rabbit or chicken. On top is a layer of small meatballs made of well-seasoned beef and pork. For Christmas the proper pie is *tourtière* (literally, pie-dish), which is made of minced pork, sometimes mixed with minced beef or veal and briefly simmered with seasonings before being enclosed in pie crust and baked *(Recipe Index).* Some recipes include mashed potatoes. *Tourtière* is usually served cold as part of the buffet after midnight Mass, but it can be served hot just as well and is better that way. Many families eat it as a treat any time of year. If a restaurant serves a single native French-Canadian dish it is likely to be *tourtière.*

Perhaps the most remarkable pie, however, is an Acadian specialty: *pâte à la râpure* (grated potato pie), which is sometimes called "rapee" pie by the Acadians' admiring English-speaking neighbors. The first step in making it is to grate about a dozen peeled potatoes. This can be done with a regular grater, but the Acadians, who grate a lot of potatoes, have something they like better. They cut the top and bottom off a very large tin can, partly flatten the cylinder and punch it full of holes with a nail. Then they nail it to a board with the sharp side of the nail-holes out. This implement grates potatoes fast. When they have all been grated, the gratings are dumped by the cupful into a clean cloth and squeezed to a dry, fluffy stuff that looks momentarily like snow.

While this is going on, a goodly amount of chicken or pork has been simmering on the stove. When the meat is tender it is removed and set aside. The broth is strained and an amount equal to the potato liquid is added to the dry potato "snow," which absorbs it completely. Then meat and broth-charged potatoes are placed in layers in a roasting pan and baked until the top is brown. *Pâte à la râpure* is like nothing else. The potato has an unexpected flavor and a texture not at all like mashed potatoes. Many Acadians claim that only Acadian women can make *pâte à la râ-*

Another time-honored Catholic feast in French Canada is *réveillon* (staying awake)—a Christmas-Eve dinner served after the family attends midnight Mass. Here the Robert Pager family, who live in Outremont, a suburb of Montreal, settle down to a candlelit meal of *bouillon de Noël,* a Christmas broth garnished with scallions *(left); croquinoles,* or doughnuts; headcheese; *tourtière,* the famous Canadian pork pie *(top) bûche de Noël,* a chocolate-covered jelly roll representing a Christmas log; and *pommes en tasse,* apples in jelly topped with whipped cream.

pure, and though it is not that hard, there must be a certain secret to it.

A pie that is French Canada's own is three-crust blueberry pie *(cipâte aux bleuets, Recipe Index).* A deep dish is lined with pastry and half filled with blueberries and sugar. The middle crust is rolled and cut to fit and then covered with the rest of the blueberries and the top crust. After baking, the middle crust is somewhat dumplinglike and suffused with delicious blueberry juice. It helps solve the problem of excess juiciness that plagues blueberry pies.

Canada shares maple sugar with the northeastern United States and is as devoted to it as Vermont or New Hampshire. It may be even more devoted. One French Canadian told me passionately: "Yes. Maple sugar is frightfully expensive. But it is indispensable, so what can you do?"

Besides the maple dishes familiar south of the border, French Canada has some of its own. Always popular are "maple grandfathers" *(grand-pères au sirop d'érable):* dumplings boiled in maple syrup and served with plenty more of the same *(Recipe Index).* An unusual breakfast dish (or dessert) that tastes much better than it sounds is eggs poached in maple syrup. There are two schools of thought about its preparation. One is to break the eggs in boiling syrup and cook them until the syrup cools; the yolks remain unbroken. But I have an emotional prejudice against liquid egg yolk mixed with maple syrup, and I prefer to have the yolks broken and stirred around a little so they solidify. The result is a delightful sweet egg dish, rather like a custard with authority.

My favorite French-Canadian dessert is also the easiest. Cut a slice of fresh white bread two thirds of an inch thick. Traditionalists insist that it be homemade bread but while this is always desirable, it is not necessary. Put it in a soup plate with plenty of maple syrup and leave it long enough to absorb all it can. Then fish it out, drain it, put it on a plate and cover it with whipped or sour cream or, better yet, sweet cream so heavy that it is almost solid. This simple dish has calories leering out of every pore, yet you will never forget it. And this is only one of many maple sugar tarts and pies (sometimes made with nuts and laced with strips of pastry) which have an intense sweetness all their own.

Modern French Canadians make a cult of wine as the French do and import a lot of it, especially from France, but their ancestors had no such elevated tastes. They distilled various homely spirits whose virtue was their alcohol, not their bouquet, and they also made wine of a sort out of the native wild grapes. A common festive drink was *caribou* (pronounced cariBOU), a mixture of home-distilled moonshine and homemade wine. Modern *caribou* is made of a special "white whiskey" sanctioned by the Canadian government, combined with Canadian red wine that looks and tastes rather like grape juice. Vodka can also be used: like white whiskey, it is ethyl alcohol and water.

In spite of its humble ingredients *caribou* is an excellent drink that is served on festive or traditional occasions. The alcoholic content is much higher than the innocent taste suggests. I asked one French Canadian why it is called *caribou.* He said: "The caribou does not look like much, but it is such a strong animal." The drink is a strong animal too; you should watch your intake of it.

Bûche de Noël *(Yule-log Cake Roll, Quebec)*

To serve 10

Preheat the oven to 350°. Brush 1 tablespoon of softened butter over the bottom and sides of a 10½-by-15½-inch jelly-roll pan. Line the pan with a 20-inch strip of wax paper and let the extra paper extend over the ends. Brush 1 tablespoon of softened butter on the paper and sprinkle it with 2 tablespoons of flour, tipping the pan from side to side. Turn the pan over and rap it sharply to remove the excess flour. Combine the 1 cup of flour, cornstarch, baking powder and salt and sift them onto a plate.

With a wire whisk or a rotary or electric beater, beat 4 of the egg whites until they begin to thicken. Slowly add ½ cup of the sugar, beating continuously until the whites are stiff enough to form unwavering peaks on the beater when it is lifted from the bowl. Beat in the vanilla.

In another bowl and with the unwashed whisk or beater, beat the egg yolks, the remaining ½ cup of sugar and the water together. When the yolk mixture thickens enough to fall from the beater in a slowly dissolving ribbon, beat in the sifted flour mixture a few tablespoons at a time. Make sure each addition is completely incorporated before beating in more. Stir ½ cup of the beaten egg whites into the yolk mixture, then scoop it over the whites and fold the two together gently but thoroughly.

Pour the batter into the lined pan and spread it evenly into the corners with a spatula. Bake in the middle of the oven for 20 minutes, or until the sides of the cake have begun to shrink away from the pan and the cake springs back instantly when pressed lightly with a fingertip.

Carefully turn the cake out on wax paper, peel the layer of paper from the top, and let it rest for 5 minutes, then spread the surface with crab-apple jelly. Starting at one long edge, roll the cake into a cylinder. Cut a 1-inch-thick slice from each end of the cake and trim each slice into a round about 1½ inches in diameter. Set the cake aside to cool.

To prepare the icing, bring the maple syrup to a boil over moderate heat in a 3- to 4-quart saucepan. Cook uncovered and undisturbed, regulating the heat to prevent the syrup from boiling over. When the syrup reaches a temperature of 238° on a candy thermometer, or when a drop spooned into ice water immediately forms a soft but compact mass, remove the pan from the heat. Add the chocolate and stir to dissolve it.

In a large bowl, beat the two remaining egg whites with a wire whisk or a rotary or electric beater until they are stiff enough to stand in unwavering peaks on the beater when it is lifted from the bowl. Beating the egg whites constantly, pour in the maple syrup-and-chocolate mixture in a slow, thin stream and continue to beat until the mixture has cooled to room temperature. Then beat in the butter bits a few pieces at a time.

When the icing is smooth and thick, spread most of it over the top, sides and ends of the cake roll with a metal spatula or knife. With fork tines, make irregular lines the length of the roll to give the icing a bark-like look and the cake the appearance of a log. Ice one side and the edges of the reserved rounds and set one on top of the log and the other on a side to resemble knotholes. Decorate the cake with holly berries made from the cherries and with leaf shapes cut from the citron.

2 tablespoons butter, softened, plus 8 tablespoons unsalted butter, softened and cut into ½-inch bits
2 tablespoons plus 1 cup flour
4 teaspoons cornstarch
1¼ teaspoons double-acting baking powder
¼ teaspoon salt
6 egg whites
1 cup sugar
½ teaspoon vanilla extract
4 egg yolks
3 tablespoons cold water
¾ cup crab-apple jelly
¾ cup pure maple syrup *(see page 161)*
1 ounce unsweetened baking chocolate, coarsely grated
Candied cherries
Candied green citron

The fern shoots *(left above)* are snipped off only a few inches long. Above, cooked fiddleheads are enhanced by a lump of melting butter. They are a sometime delicacy, for the fresh fiddlehead season is extremely short—in New Brunswick, about 10 days.

who know its history. Some dishes, including the irrepressible shepherd's pie of England (a minced-meat pie with a mashed potato top) are unchanged immigrants while others such as Indian pudding came intact from New England. But the cooks of the Maritimes have a way of modifying even the simplest dishes. Jonnycake, for instance, which in its classic New England version contains nothing but corn meal, hot water and salt, turned into something entirely different by the time it got to Prince Edward Island. There it has twice as much flour as corn meal, along with eggs, shortening, baking powder and milk and maple syrup. It emerges from the oven a sort of sweet bread with a little corn meal in it. Another New England creation that underwent a sea change on the way to P.E.I. is steamed brown bread. The island version does not use corn meal, rye meal and whole wheat flour in equal parts as tradition dictates; it substitutes bran and white flour. As a New Englander I have a tendency to denounce this as heresy or even desecration, but perhaps I should honor it as creativity. There may be islanders who think they invented brown bread. They are self-assured people; it is said that when little Prince Edward Island joined the Canadian Federation in 1873 one of its citizens claimed that Canada was joining them.

As in most vigorous northern countries many dishes in the Maritimes are not for weight-watching women or desk-bound men. A conspicuous example is farmer's breakfast, compounded in a frying pan of bacon, cut-up boiled potatoes, chopped onion, grated cheese and eggs. The trick is first to fry the bacon crisp and take it out. Then pour off part of the bacon grease (how much to remove is a matter of taste) and slightly brown the

potatoes and onion in the remainder. Restore the crisp bacon and sprinkle with cheese. Next break a lot of eggs on top and cook them gently without stirring until the whites are firm. The dish is great, but takes a morning of plowing or wood chopping to work it off. It is best in a womanless environment such as a hunting camp.

Not all Maritime food is as calorific, but there is usually a tendency in that energizing direction. Fish and shellfish chowders and stews tend to have more butter in them than they do in New England. A potato and sausage casserole is graced with butter to aggravate the already ample fat that comes from the sausages. Fresh, fragrant, home-baked bread is a common temptation, and most households that can afford it, as most can, are always stocked with rich homemade cookies, cakes and shortbreads. One time-honored molasses cake is made with equal amounts of flour and fresh ground fat pork. Pies, sweet puddings and sweet pudding sauces are all over the place while salads and green low-calorie vegetables are not emphasized. However repugnant this may seem to modern urban kitchen mores, it is appropriate for the Maritimes where cities are few and small and most men lead outdoor or semi-outdoor lives in a boisterous climate. Perhaps the women manage to diet in the face of this blizzard of delectable dishes, or perhaps they, like the men, live physically active lives. In any case only a few are more than pleasantly plump.

Most Maritime cookbooks have a section on supper dishes, which are fairly light fare by local standards. One attractive dish (I suspect of Lunenberg German origin) is made of pancakes stacked up with a filling be-

As dories of the local oyster fleet bob behind him on the waters of Prince Edward Island *(far left)*, James A. Beaton, an oyster fisherman for more than 30 years, displays some of his catch and an essential tool of his trade: long tongs of wood and metal used to lift the oysters from their shallow beds. Malpeque oysters are famous for their plumpness and matchless flavor, which islanders say is due to the fact that they grow faster than any other oyster. At left, a half dozen Malpeques are ready to eat, just as they come from the sea.

tween them and served in wedges like pie. The top pancake is heavily buttered to keep it from burning and the stack is baked until the eggs mixed in the filling solidify. The filling may also contain seafood, mushrooms, chopped ham or any other leftover meat. When served as dessert, pancakes are rolled up with a filling of egg, cottage cheese or jam and cooked enough to heat them through.

When cooking fish and other seafood, which are cheap, good and easily come by, the cooks of the Maritimes show commendable originality. Besides the dishes common in New England, they have developed any number of others that most New Englanders never heard of, such as fish loaves analogous to meat loaves. They make fish "jelly rolls" with biscuit dough, cut them in slices, lay them flat and bake them. They dip fish fillets in thick batter and fry them crisp in deep fat. Another of their excellent ways of cooking fillets is to bake them covered with a sauce made of milk, butter, mustard and grated cheese. This turns even the driest fish, such as long-frozen halibut, into a most agreeable meal.

Lobsters are somewhat less expensive in parts of the Maritimes than in the United States and so are still used with some abandon. They are creamed, cooked in casserole dishes, scalloped, fried or baked *(Recipe Index)*. A variation new to me is a lobster chowder made by frying raw lobster meat in butter until it turns red on the outside. This gives a different and interesting flavor but must be considerably more trouble.

Lobsters are important in the Maritimes as a money-earning export, but the time when they were cheap and abundant is still in the recent past

Continued on page 193

189

The ingredients Aunt Maud uses in preparing fish and brewis are potatoes, onion, salt cod, fat-back pork and hardtack.

"Fish and Brewis" Cooked in the Newfoundland Way

Daughter of one cod fisherman and widow of another, Mrs. Maud Lear spent summers in her girlhood cooking for fishermen on their trips to Labrador. Here, at home at Hibbs Cove, Newfoundland, Aunt Maud (as she is known to everyone around) makes her version of fish and brewis: she uses salt cod and adds hardtack, potatoes, onions and fat-back pork. Right, she peels the skin from the cod. She cuts the fish in pieces and soaks it and the hardtack, separately, overnight. The next morning she changes the water on the cod, boils it 20 minutes, drains it and removes the bones. She brings the hardtack to boil in its soaking water, then drains it. At far right, at her wood-burning stove, she mixes the boiled cod with softened hardtack and boiled potatoes. In the iron pot are fried onions and scrunchions (bits of pork fat). Aunt Maud serves this separately like a gravy.

190

One of Newfoundland's finest delicacies, fried cod tongues, is shown as prepared by Aunt Maud Lear. First, she rolls the tongues in flour seasoned with salt and pepper. Below, she drops them into hot fat rendered from salt pork. She fries them for 12 minutes on each side, until they turn light brown. At right, they are served by the glow of a kerosene lantern. The taste of cod tongues is rich yet delicate, but they must be eaten on the same day the fish are caught; otherwise the tongues turn tough and glutinous.

and so they are not worshipped as piously as in the United States. The most appreciated shellfish is the Digby scallop which is caught six fathoms deep in the Digby Cut, an ultra-cold part of the Bay of Fundy. Like a small sea scallop, its shell is flatter, larger and heavier than those of the American bay scallop and not fluted or scalloped. The meats are made into chowders and soups, baked in white sauce or scalloped in a baking dish with cream and bread or cracker crumbs *(Recipe Index)*. Perhaps the most attractive way to serve them is to place three or four scallop meats on each scallop shell and surround them with a circle of mashed potatoes squeezed out like cake frosting. Put a dab of butter in the center and sprinkle lightly with bread crumbs, salt and pepper. Then bake until scallops and potato are lightly browned. Diced boiled potato is sometimes used, but it does not hold the butter and scallop juice as efficiently.

Another species of shellfish has begun to rival the Digby scallop. Until recently hardly anyone knew that the queen crab existed, but the creature was there all the time in 300 feet or more of water, notably in the eastern part of the Gulf of Saint Lawrence. A few years ago a new kind of trawl began bringing up crabs with small bodies and wide-spreading legs, somewhat like the king crabs of the North Pacific but smaller. Their flesh was delicious and easily marketable, so resourceful fishermen devised a way to catch them in quantity. They built large traps of welded steel rods and nylon netting that work on the principle of lobster pots, and sank them in water of the proper depth. Up came rich catches of crabs, the joints of whose unwieldy legs yield finger-shaped pieces of white flesh that I have found more tender and better flavored than king crab.

Queen crab is too new to have acquired special cooking methods. It hardly needs them. Simply broiled with butter it is marvelous. The body meat, which comes in small pieces, can be chopped or flaked like any crab meat, but the choice fingers from the legs should be kept intact.

The luxury fish of the Maritimes is the Atlantic salmon, which is baked, steamed, fried, stewed, broiled *(Restigouche salmon, Recipe Index)* made into pie or chowder or soused in vinegar. The most lordly salmon dish of all—known on the West Coast as well as the East—is fresh planked salmon, said by some to have originated with the Indians. A whole salmon is split down the back and the backbone removed, taking with it most of the small bones attached to it. The rest can be felt in the flesh and pulled out with pliers. The head, viscera and tail are also removed, and the fish is sprinkled with salt and closed for two hours to let the salt work its way into the flesh. Then the fish is nailed to a hardwood (not a resiny softwood) plank, using large-headed roofing nails to hold it securely. It is sprinkled lightly with flour and stood on end beside a blazing camp fire until it is lightly browned, which takes about 20 minutes depending on the vigor of the flame. If the fire smokes as most camp fires do, so much the better; smoke in moderation improves the flavor. When done, the fish is laid flat for serving and doused with butter. The flesh easily comes away from the skin with a fork and is glorious eating, Indians or no Indians.

The best large stretch of good farmland in the Maritimes is Prince Edward Island, which is flat, free of rock outcrops and cultivated almost solidly from beach to beach. Its Micmac Indian name was Abegweit, which is said to mean "the home cradled in the waves," which is a little puzzling because the Indians had no cradles and, since they drew no maps, were not likely to have appreciated its cradlelike shape. The French called it Saint Jean, and the British eventually renamed it after Queen Victoria's father. The big crop is potatoes, and the islanders have some pleasant ways of cooking them. One of the best is crusty potato logs, which are mashed potatoes, butter and egg yolks flavored with a touch of thyme, shaped into small cylinders, rolled in beaten egg and crushed dry cereal or cracker crumbs and baked until crisp. Another is called shepherd's pie, but is not like the English version. It is a real pie with meat, gravy and diced potatoes and other vegetables, covered with pastry crust, which makes it an attractive variation of the English original.

In Nova Scotia the best farming section is the Annapolis Valley on the Bay of Fundy. It is famous for apples, which it exports in great quantities to much of the world, and for attractive ways of cooking them. Apple eating starts at breakfast with apple pancakes made with sliced or grated apples, fried apples with sausages or baked apples stuffed with chopped ham. It continues through all the courses of the other meals. Apples are mixed in breads, muffins and cakes, added to baked dishes, used in poultry stuffing and cooked with almost any meat or seafood. Fried apples are great favorites. The apples should be cored but not peeled, cut in slices about a third of an inch thick, sprinkled with sugar and fried until brown. The rings of skin keep them from coming apart.

Annapolis Valley cooks really let themselves go with apple desserts. One collection of recipes lists 14 ways to make apple pie, eight kinds of apple pudding and any number of unclassifiable sweet apple dishes. My favorite is an apple upside-down pie (or cake) with plenty of butter and sugar, topped with meringue. It should be made, I am told, only with high-quality, slightly tart cooking apples, preferably Gravensteins.

Cape Breton, in Nova Scotia, is the Scottish center. It has a Gaelic college where the Gaelic language is taught, kilts are worn, bagpipes are skirled and robust Scottish pastimes such as tossing the caber (throwing small telephone poles) are encouraged. True to the custom of the homeland, the cuisine features oats, which besides being served in the traditional porridge, form the basis of various kinds of breads and cakes. One good one is oatcakes made with scarcely any liquid at all *(Recipe Index)*, oatmeal (not rolled oats), butter and a little sugar, rolled thin, baked and cut in squares. I was warned about local versions of the Scottish haggis (a sheep's stomach stuffed with oatmeal, ground sheep's innards and seasonings, and boiled), but did not meet with any.

I feel that Newfoundland deserves separate treatment here because it is such a very separate place. Standing far out in the Atlantic, it has the feeling of a ship at sea, or rather a flotilla of ships, for each small town, village or cluster of houses hugs its own harbor. Each deals with the sea individually as a ship does, and has little to do with its neighbors or the wilderness a few miles behind the shore. In many of the smaller seaside villages (locally called "outports") the hardy people speak a blend of English dialects peculiar to themselves. Philologists who have studied these fossil dialects believe that some of them preserve the speech of English seamen of 300 years ago.

Nearly everyone up in Newfoundland (pronounced Newfound*land*) makes his living directly or indirectly from the sea. There is little agriculture. Minerals and papermaking are of secondary importance, and the big American-run radar establishments lead isolated lives of their own. The provincial capital, Saint John's, has an almost ideal harbor whose entrance is a narrow cleft in a line of steep, sheltering hills. Usually it has plenty of room, but when radio stations far to the south shout warnings of a storm at sea, it fills up rapidly. From the Grand Banks, the famous ocean fishing ground that lies southeast of Saint John's, comes a parade of fishing boats running for refuge. Some of them are schooners that look as if they had sailed out of an earlier age. Others are large and modern. They fly many flags: Spanish, Portuguese, French, English, Norwegian, Icelandic, East and West German, Russian and Polish. They tie up in clusters at the wharves, sometimes crowding all suitable space, and their men swarm ashore to tramp the streets of Saint John's. They are almost always orderly, especially the Russians, who move in tight, solemn groups with wondering, round blue eyes.

Traditional Newfoundland cooking is circumscribed by the fact that almost everything except seafood must come from across the water from Canada or Europe. In the old days of slow sailing ships and no airplanes this meant that most beef was corned beef (the "salt horse" of seamen). Salt pork, both lean and fat, was also a staple, and the commonest fruits were dates and raisins. Modern transportation and ways of freezing and canning have brought a greater variety and abundance, but the old-fashioned dishes based on foods that sailing vessels could carry without spoilage are still popular, and many of them are surprisingly good.

Newfoundland's staff of life is "fish and brewis" (pronounced brews). Fish means codfish (salt or fresh) unless otherwise specified, and brewis is the hard bread of the age of sail. No one who has not seen it and tried to eat it can believe how hard it is. It comes in boat-shaped biscuits three inches long, one and a half inches broad, one and a half inches thick, and literally as hard as wood. They are not meant to be eaten without long soaking, but children are often given one of them to moisten and chew on. It lasts all day.

The classic directions for cooking fish and brewis on a fishing boat are as follows, from a contemporary Newfoundland cook: "Cut a quarter of a pound of fat back pork into very small pieces and put it in a bake-pot over medium heat and cook until all the fat is rendered out of the pork, leaving the fat and scrunchions [cracklings] in the bottom of the pot. While pork is cooking, go on deck with a cod-jigger and catch a medium-size codfish and remove head, tail, skin and guts. Wash in clean water from the side of the boat, then cut in three or four pieces and place them in the bake-pot with the fat and scrunchions and cook from 15 to 20 minutes, or until it is cooked, then remove all bones. Take a half-pound of hard bread, place it in a piece of ship's canvas or calico and beat with a hammer or the head of an axe until it becomes very small and powdery. Then throw it in the bake-pot with the fish, scrunchions and fat, and mix through and through until all the vitamins from the juice of the fish have been mixed with the bread crumbs. Serve piping hot for three or four people, and you have *some* meal."

People who do not pull their codfish out of the ocean while the scrunchions are browning can get them elsewhere, but Newfoundlanders are always fussy about their fish. They prefer, for instance, codfish whose backs are almost black, caught in certain localities. When salt cod is used it is soaked overnight. Hard biscuits are split in two and soaked also. Then both fish and brewis are boiled briefly and drained. They are served on a platter with potatoes and cut-up onions mixed in, and with the pork fat and scrunchions in a separate bowl to pour over them. Try this archaic dish sometime for a pleasant surprise.

In Newfoundland salt cod is big business, and it is cured in many different ways. The fish are first split and packed in salt to remove much of the water in the flesh. For the American market, the fish often is dried artificially indoors, which produces a white or slightly gray product. For markets in southern Europe or Latin America—where this food is very popular—the Newfoundlanders sun dry their salt cod on wooden platforms much as was done 300 years ago. The flesh turns yellow or even brown, but this is what the customers like. Shipments for Spain, Italy, Greece or Brazil must be treated in special ways or they may not sell.

My guess is that Newfoundland has more ways to cook fish, either fresh or salt, than anywhere else in the world. An excellent way to make an attractive dish out of any kind of fish fillets is to spread them thinly with a bread-crumb filling flavored not too strongly with grated onion and summer savory, which is Newfoundland's favorite herb and is grown there. The fillets are then rolled up, coated with flour and browned in fat. They can be eaten as is, but are good baked in a casserole with cream sauce topped with buttered crumbs.

Another good and distinctive dish is fish baked in custard. The fillets are simmered with milk in a baking dish until tender. Then the milk is drained off and combined with butter and beaten eggs, poured back on the fish and the dish is baked. A third way is to pile up four buttered fillets, wrap in foil with the edges up to hold the juices, and bake.

Though cod is the premier fish—the seafood staff-of-life—Newfoundland has innumerable other fish, some of which, such as the Greenland turbot, are unfamiliar farther south. Eels are seldom eaten, but they are flown to eel-loving Germany to sell for high prices. Salmon is plentiful in season; it is sometimes baked under a blanket of butter, flour and mustard. In summer enormous schools of capelin, a small, smeltlike fish, appear offshore surrounded by schools of larger fish delightedly feeding on them. In the rush to spawning grounds, they sometimes pile up so thick that the water is almost solid with them. Anyone can have all he wants merely by dipping them out of the water. The few farmers who cultivate Newfoundland's difficult soil drive wagons into the surf and fill them with capelins, which they usually spread as fertilizer.

Capelins are delicious when sautéed; they have a delicate, unusual flavor and hardly any bones, but they are a sorrow for Newfoundland's entrepreneurs, who have tried without success to establish a market for them. The great bluefin tuna, which are sometimes boated up to 1,000 pounds, are another source of frustration. They are canned, of course, but there is little demand for them as fresh fish. The Newfoundlanders maintain that this is because no one knows how to cook them. Tuna is oily, it has some of the texture of meat and it does not get tender, as other fish do, when briefly fried or boiled. It should be roasted like beef. Get a solid chunk four inches thick and soak it in milk overnight. Put it on a cake rack so it will not sit in its own oil and bake it for 1½ hours. Then cut off the bottom inch where oil has accumulated and serve the rest.

Newfoundland lacks the climate for growing vintage wine, but nevertheless it has a kind of port of which it is proud. In 1679 an English ship laden with port wine was heading home from Portugal. While crossing the Bay of Biscay, it was pursued by French privateers and fled out into the Atlantic. The weather was bad and stores were low, so the captain ran for Newfoundland and took refuge in the cozy harbor of Newman's plantation, now Saint John's, where the port was unloaded and stored for the winter. In spring it was taken to London where connoisseurs hailed it as the world's best port, matured by the tossing of two Atlantic crossings. Ever since then Newman's Port has been brought to Saint John's and stored in rock-cut cellars before being sent to London. Even halfway through its journey it is capital port.

Another Newfoundland drink is a notably powerful medium dark rum. When Newfoundland joined Canada in 1948, the rum's potency had to be reduced to conform to federal rules, but it is still dynamite. Part of its punch may come from the shock effect of its name: Screech.

In all the Maritime Provinces (except Prince Edward Island, which is too completely cultivated) game is an important part of the cuisine, not merely an interesting novelty to talk about. Moose are almost too plentiful, sometimes wandering into suburban backyards. Recently a large bull established residence at the Saint John's airport and had to be shot as a hazard on the runways. A 400-pound moose is a lot of meat, so during and after hunting season many people are concerned with how to cook it.

Most experts advise hanging moose meat like beef to tenderize it a bit. Even so it is likely to be tough. Only the tenderest parts of especially tender moose, such as cuts from the loin, should be fried as steaks, and since the meat has no fat of its own these should be served with plenty of fried onions and scrunchions. Tougher meat is best cooked as stew, pot roast or mooseburger. Deer venison is tenderer and so is caribou.

In Newfoundland the moose and caribou that share the unpeopled interior may soon be joined by buffalo. A few years ago wildlife experts made a study of what the native game animals eat. They found that the moose live largely on palm (not a palm tree but a low bush, pronounced pam) while caribou prefer lichens. No sizable animal eats the grass that covers some areas. This seemed a waste, so the government imported a few buffalo from western Canada and released them on an island off the southern shore. They thrived in the stormy but not very cold climate. When the experts are satisfied that the buffalo will not interfere with moose or caribou, they will be released to multiply on the main island. Then the Newfoundlanders will start figuring how to cook buffalo.

Fried Cod Tongues *(Newfoundland)*

To serve 4 to 6

1 pound fresh cod tongues
1 tablespoon strained fresh lemon
    juice
¾ cup flour
½ teaspoon salt
Freshly ground black pepper
¼ pound lean salt pork with rind
    removed, the pork cut into
    ¼-inch dice

Wash the cod tongues in a sieve or colander under cold running water and pat them completely dry with paper towels. Sprinkle the tongues evenly with the lemon juice and spread them side by side on a piece of wax paper. Combine the flour, salt and a few grindings of pepper in a large paper bag and set aside.

In a heavy 12-inch skillet, fry the salt pork over moderate heat, turning the dice about frequently with a slotted spoon until they are crisp and brown and have rendered all their fat. Scoop out and discard the dice.

Drop the cod tongues into the flour mixture and shake the bag vigorously to coat them on all sides. Then, one at a time, shake the excess flour off the tongues and arrange them in one layer in the fat remaining in the skillet. Fry uncovered over moderately low heat for about 10 minutes on each side, or until delicately browned.

Drain the tongues briefly on paper towels and serve them at once from a heated platter. Traditionally, fried cod tongues are accompanied by boiled turnips and potatoes.

Baked Stuffed Lobster *(Nova Scotia)*

To serve 2

A 2½- to 3-pound live lobster
8 tablespoons butter, plus 10
    tablespoons butter melted, plus 2
    tablespoons butter, cut into
    ¼-inch bits
½ teaspoon finely chopped garlic
1½ cups soft fresh crumbs made
    from homemade-type white
    bread, pulverized in a blender or
    finely shredded with a fork
2 tablespoons finely cut fresh chives
2 tablespoons finely chopped fresh
    parsley
2 tablespoons dry sherry
½ teaspoon salt
Freshly ground black pepper
1 lemon cut in quarters

Ask your fish dealer to split the lobster for you, or do it yourself in the following fashion: Lay the lobster on its back on a chopping board and, with a kitchen towel wrapped around one hand for protection, grasp the lobster firmly. With a large, heavy, sharp knife, cut the body and tail lengthwise in half.

Remove and discard the gelatinous sac (stomach) in the head of the lobster and the long white intestinal vein which is attached to it, but leave the greenish-brown tomalley (liver) and the black caviarlike eggs (coral), if any, in place. (See the photographs on page 108.) Gash the flat side of each large claw with a knife.

In a heavy 10- to 12-inch skillet, melt 8 tablespoons of butter over moderate heat. When the foam begins to subside, add the garlic and stir for a minute or so. Then add the bread crumbs and, stirring frequently, fry until they are golden brown. Remove the skillet from the heat and stir in the chives, parsley, sherry, salt and a few grindings of pepper. Taste the stuffing mixture for seasoning.

With a pastry brush, spread 2 tablespoons of the melted butter evenly over the exposed tail meat. Spoon the stuffing mixture into the cavities in both halves of the body of the lobster. Arrange the lobster halves in a shallow baking dish large enough to hold them comfortably. Then dot the stuffing with the 2 tablespoons of butter bits.

Bake the lobster on the middle shelf of the oven for about 30 minutes, or until the stuffing is golden.

Serve the lobster at once, directly from the baking dish or arranged attractively on a heated platter. Garnish the lobster with the lemon quarters. Pour the remaining 8 tablespoons of melted butter into individual sauce bowls and present it separately with the lobster.

Chocolate Bread Pudding (Nova Scotia)

Mix the bread crumbs and milk in a deep bowl and let them soak at room temperature for 30 minutes, stirring from time to time.

Meanwhile, preheat the oven to 350°. With a pastry brush, spread the softened butter evenly over the bottom and sides of a 6-cup soufflé or baking dish. Set aside.

In a heavy 2- to 3-quart saucepan, melt the chocolate over low heat, stirring frequently to prevent it from burning. Remove from the heat and add the sugar. Then, stirring the chocolate mixture constantly, pour in the bread crumbs and milk in a slow thin stream. When the ingredients are well blended, beat in the eggs and add the vanilla.

Pour into the buttered dish and bake the pudding in the middle of the oven for 2 hours, or until the top is a deep crusty brown and a knife inserted in the center comes out clean.

Serve the pudding at once, accompanied by a pitcher of heavy cream.

To serve 6

2 cups soft fresh crumbs made from homemade-type white bread, pulverized in a blender or finely shredded with a fork
1 quart milk
1 tablespoon butter, softened
2 one-ounce squares unsweetened baking chocolate
⅔ cup sugar
2 eggs, lightly beaten
½ teaspoon vanilla extract
Heavy cream

Oat Bread (Newfoundland)

Pour the water into a small bowl and sprinkle the yeast and sugar over it. Let stand for 2 or 3 minutes, then stir well. Set in a warm, draft-free place (such as an unlighted oven) for about 10 minutes, or until the yeast bubbles up and the mixture almost doubles in volume. Meanwhile, combine the milk, molasses, 2 tablespoons of butter and the salt in a small saucepan and, stirring occasionally, cook over moderate heat until bubbles begin to form around the edges of the pan. Pour the milk mixture into a deep bowl and set aside to cool to lukewarm.

Add the yeast and the oats to the milk mixture and stir together with a wooden spoon. Then add 3 cups of the flour, 1 cup at a time, and continue to stir until the dough can be gathered into a medium-soft ball.

Place the ball on a lightly floured surface and knead, pushing the dough down with the heels of your hands, pressing it forward and folding it back on itself. As you knead, incorporate up to 2 cups more flour, sprinkling it over the ball by the tablespoonful and adding only enough to make a non-sticky dough. Knead for about 10 minutes, or until the dough is smooth, shiny and elastic. Then reshape it into a ball.

With a pastry brush, spread 2 teaspoons of softened butter evenly inside a deep mixing bowl. Place the ball in the bowl and turn it around to butter the entire surface of the dough. Drape the bowl loosely with a kitchen towel and put it in the draft-free place for about 1½ hours, or until the dough doubles in volume.

Brush the remaining 2 teaspoons of softened butter over the bottoms and sides of two 9-by-5-inch loaf tins. Punch the dough down with a single blow of your fist and divide it in half. On a lightly floured surface pat and shape each half into a loaf. Place the dough in the pans and brush the top of each loaf with the melted butter. Drape a kitchen towel over the loaves and set them aside to rise again for about 30 minutes, or until doubled in bulk.

Preheat the oven to 375°. Bake the loaves on the middle shelf of the oven for 40 to 45 minutes, or until they are light brown. Turn out the bread on wire racks and cool to room temperature before serving.

To make two 9-by-5-inch loaves

½ cup lukewarm water (110° to 115°)
1 package active dry yeast
1 teaspoon sugar
2 cups milk
½ cup dark molasses
2 tablespoons butter plus 4 teaspoons butter, softened, plus 2 tablespoons butter, melted
2 teaspoons salt
2 cups regular rolled oats (not the quick-cooking variety)
4 to 5 cups flour

To serve 4

¼ cup vegetable oil
3 tablespoons strained fresh lemon
    juice
1 teaspoon finely grated lemon peel
1 tablespoon finely chopped
    scallions, white part only
¼ teaspoon crumbled dried
    marjoram
½ teaspoon salt
⅛ teaspoon freshly ground black
    pepper
Four 8- to 10-ounce salmon steaks,
    cut about 1 inch thick
1 tablespoon butter, softened, plus 4
    tablespoons butter, melted
2 lemons, cut lengthwise into
    quarters

To serve 6

8 to 11 tablespoons butter
6 thin slices homemade-type white
    bread, cut into 3-inch rounds
    with a cookie cutter or the rim of
    a glass
2 tablespoons freshly grated onions
1 pound fresh wild Tantramar
    mushrooms, or substitute 1 pound
    fresh cultivated mushrooms,
    trimmed, wiped with a damp
    cloth, and cut lengthwise into
    ⅓-inch-thick slices
2 teaspoons strained fresh lemon
    juice
2 tablespoons flour
1 cup chicken stock, fresh or canned
½ cup light cream
1 teaspoon celery seed
1 teaspoon salt
¼ teaspoon freshly ground black
    pepper
2 tablespoons finely chopped parsley

Restigouche Salmon (New Brunswick)

The Restigouche River, between New Brunswick and the Gaspé Peninsula, is famous for its large Atlantic salmon.

Combine the oil, lemon juice, lemon peel, scallions, marjoram, salt and pepper in a shallow baking dish large enough to hold the salmon steaks in one layer. Beat the marinade ingredients together with a whisk, then add the salmon steaks and turn them over to coat them evenly on both sides. Marinate the steaks at room temperature for 20 to 30 minutes, turning them once or twice.

Preheat the broiler to the highest possible setting. Just before broiling the salmon, remove the broiler pan from the oven and, with a pastry brush, spread the tablespoon of softened butter on the broiler grill.

Arrange the salmon steaks side by side on the grill and spoon the marinade over them. Basting the steaks every 2 minutes or so with the melted butter, broil them 4 inches from the heat for 5 to 7 minutes on each side, or until they are a golden brown and the fish feels firm when prodded gently with a finger.

To serve, transfer the salmon to a heated platter and arrange the lemon wedges around the fish.

Tantramar Mushrooms (New Brunswick)

Tantramar mushrooms, which grow wild around the marshes outside of Sackville, New Brunswick, at the head of the Bay of Fundy, are thought to have been planted originally by early French settlers.

Preheat the oven to its lowest setting. Line a baking pan with a double thickness of paper towels and place it on the middle shelf of the oven.

In a heavy 12-inch skillet, melt 3 tablespoons of the butter over moderate heat. When the foam begins to subside, add the bread rounds. Turn them with a slotted spatula and regulate the heat so that they color richly and evenly on both sides without burning. If necessary, add up to 3 tablespoons more butter to the skillet, a tablespoonful at a time. When the bread rounds are done, transfer them to the paper-lined pan and keep them warm in the oven while you prepare the mushrooms.

In the same skillet melt the remaining butter over moderate heat. Drop in the onions and stir for 1 or 2 minutes until they are soft but not brown. Add the mushrooms and, stirring occasionally, fry them for 8 to 10 minutes, or until almost all the liquid that accumulates in the pan has evaporated. Do not let the mushrooms brown.

Add the lemon juice and stir in the flour. Then, stirring the mixture constantly with a wire whisk, pour in the chicken stock and the cream in a slow, thin stream and cook over high heat until the sauce comes to a boil, thickens lightly and is smooth. Add the celery seed, salt and pepper, reduce the heat to low and simmer for 5 minutes to remove the raw taste of the flour. Taste for seasoning.

Arrange the fried bread rounds attractively on a heated platter or individual plates and spoon about ½ cup of the mushroom mixture over each one. Sprinkle with chopped parsley and serve at once.

Stuffed Baked Potatoes *(Prince Edward Island)*

To serve 6

Preheat the oven to 425°. With a pastry brush, spread 2 tablespoons of the softened butter evenly over the skins of the potatoes. Bake the potatoes on a rack in the middle of the oven for about 1 hour. The potatoes are done if they feel soft when squeezed gently between your thumb and forefinger. Remove the potatoes and reduce the oven temperature to 400°.

Meanwhile, in a heavy 10- to 12-inch skillet, fry the bacon over moderate heat, turning the slices frequently with tongs until they are crisp and brown. Drain the bacon on paper towels, crumble it into small bits and set aside. Brush 1 tablespoon of softened butter over the bottom of a shallow baking dish large enough to hold the potatoes in one layer.

Cut a ¼-inch-thick lengthwise slice off the top of each baked potato. With a spoon, scoop out the potato pulp, leaving the skin intact and creating a boatlike shell about ¼ inch thick.

Place the potato pulp in a deep bowl and mash it into a smooth purée with the back of a fork, or rub the pulp through a ricer into a deep bowl. Add the remaining 4 tablespoons of softened butter, the grated cheese, milk, salt and pepper and beat vigorously until the mixture is smooth. Stir in the bacon bits and the scallions and taste for seasoning.

Spoon the potato mixture into the shells, mounding it in the center. Arrange the shells in the buttered dish and sprinkle the butter bits on top. Bake in the middle of the oven until the potatoes are golden brown and crusty. Serve at once.

7 tablespoons butter, softened, plus 1 tablespoon butter, cut into ¼-inch bits
6 eight-ounce baking potatoes, thoroughly scrubbed and patted dry with paper towels
6 slices (about 4 ounces) lean bacon
¾ cup freshly grated sharp Cheddar cheese
½ cup milk
1 teaspoon salt
¼ teaspoon freshly ground black pepper
2 tablespoons finely chopped scallions, white part only

Cape Breton Scones *(Nova Scotia)*

To make 12 two-inch square scones

Preheat the oven to 450°. With a pastry brush, spread the teaspoon of softened butter evenly over a large baking sheet. In a bowl beat the eggs with a wire whisk or fork. When they are well beaten, measure 2 tablespoons of the eggs and set them aside in a saucer.

Combine 3½ cups of the flour, the sugar, baking powder and salt and sift them into a deep bowl. Add the 12 tablespoons of butter bits and, with your fingertips, rub the mixture together until it resembles flakes of coarse meal. Make a well in the center and into it pour the beaten eggs and the milk. With a spoon, gradually incorporate the dry ingredients into the liquid ones, then beat vigorously until the dough is smooth and can be gathered into a soft ball.

Place the ball on a lightly floured surface and knead, pushing the dough down with the heels of your hands, pressing it forward and folding it back on itself. As you knead, incorporate up to ½ cup more flour, sprinkling it in by the tablespoonful and using only enough to make a firm, non-sticky dough.

Roll the dough into a rectangle about 8 inches long, 6 inches wide and ¾ inch thick. Brush the top with the reserved 2 tablespoons of egg and sprinkle it with brown sugar. With a pastry wheel or a knife dipped in flour, cut the dough into 2-inch squares. Then, lifting them with a metal spatula, arrange the squares 1 inch apart on the buttered baking sheet.

Bake in the middle of the oven for about 15 minutes until the scones are puffed, brown and firm to the touch. Serve at once, accompanied if you like by sweet butter and jam.

1 teaspoon butter, softened, plus 12 tablespoons butter, chilled and cut into ¼-inch bits
2 eggs
4 cups flour
¼ cup sugar
2 tablespoons double-acting baking powder
½ teaspoon salt
1 cup milk
⅓ cup dark brown sugar

Recipe Index: English

NOTE: An R preceding a page refers to the Recipe Booklet. Size, weight and material are specified for pans in the recipes because they affect cooking results. A pan should be just large enough to hold its contents comfortably. Heavy pans heat slowly and cook food at a constant rate. Aluminum and cast iron conduct heat well but may discolor foods containing egg yolks, wine, vinegar or lemon. Enamelware is a fairly poor conductor of heat. Many recipes therefore recommend stainless steel or enameled cast iron, which do not have these faults.

INGREDIENTS: Most of the ingredients called for in this book's recipes can be found at any grocery or supermarket. Few recipes include products that are not widely available. Cod cheeks and tongues and fresh herring roe and milt are rarely found outside some coastal areas of New England and Canada. Beach plums grow wild along the North Atlantic seaboard and seldom appear in markets anywhere. Boiled cider, pure maple syrup and maple sugar are Vermont specialties; for information about ordering them by mail write to the Vermont Development Department, Montpelier, Vermont 05602.

Recipe Index: French Canadian

General Index